PICTURES & WORDS TOGETHER

CHILDREN ILLUSTRATING AND WRITING THEIR OWN BOOKS

PAUL JOHNSON

HEINEMANN

PORTSMOUTH, NH

HEINEMANN
A division of Reed Elsevier Inc.
361 Hanover Street
Portsmouth, NH 03801-3912

Offices and agents throughout the world

A shortened version of Chapter 1 first appeared in *Reading* 28 (3). Excerpts from Chapter 7 appeared in *The Journal of Art and Design Education* 13 (1).

The author would like to thank the headteachers and staff of the Beaver Road Infant and Junior School, Didsbury, Manchester, and Birchfields Primary School, Rusholme, Manchester, for their assistance in making this book possible.

Library of Congress Cataloging-in-Publication Data

Johnson, Paul, 1943–
　　Pictures and words together : children illustrating and writing
　　　　their own books / Paul Johnson.
　　　　p.　cm.
　　Includes bibliographical references.
　　ISBN 0-435-08883-1 (alk. paper).
　　1. Illustration of books—Study and teaching (Preschool)
2. English language—Composition and exercises—Study and teaching
(Preschool)　3. Child authors.　4. Kindergarten.　I. Title.
LB 1140.5.A7J65　1997
372.5'2—dc20　　　　　　　　　　　　　　　　　　96-44623
　　　　　　　　　　　　　　　　　　　　　　　　　　　CIP

Editor: Carolyn Coman
Production: Vicki Kasabian
Text design: Joni Doherty
Cover design: Jenny Jensen Greenleaf
Manufacturing: Louise Richardson

Printed in the United States of American on acid-free paper

Docutech T & C 2004

To

MARIA PIA ALIGNANI

◆

A book starts with an idea.

ALIKI

———

♦

Words evoke. Illustrations present.

MALLARME

———

Contents

Introduction

It has been asserted that we are entering a historical epoch in which the image will take over from the written word. In view of this claim it is all the more important to clarify the potentialities of the image in communication, to ask what it can and what it cannot do better than spoken or written language.   —E. H. GOMBRICH

I firmly believe children should be taught to write and illustrate their writing as an interrelated process. Although the emphasis in this book is on helping students develop illustration skills, writing and art are so organically and culturally interrelated that the two must be discussed together. What do children learn from illustrating their texts? How do texts and illustrations "work" together?

Art Is Everywhere

Children may use many forms of drawing in a school week—a formal art lesson, diagrams and charts in history and science projects, sketches in notebooks and journals. In some contexts, drawing is an add-on activity, a reward for completing an assignment: students who have finished a piece of narrative writing are often encouraged to make a drawing "to go with it." And in the uncharted waters of the hidden curriculum, pupils doodle on the covers and in the margins of their workbooks, on containers and bags, inside school desks, even on the palms and backs of their hands!

Meaning in Pictures

It is often said that the young rehearse writing through their drawings, but art must not be seen as merely a surrogate for words. Visual communication dominates our lives both in the workplace and at leisure. In fact, this book looks at just one small aspect of it—children turning their narrative texts into illustrated books.

Just as film and TV integrate the spoken word and moving pictures, an illustrated book integrates the written word and still pictures. Both forms of communication are dynamic modes of defining and understanding.

Meaning in Story

As Eric Carlin (1986) says, the form of writing children overwhelmingly prefer is the story, especially science fiction or other kinds of fantasy. These stories are exciting to write, engage the students in a world of their own making, and provide intrinsic rewards for the writer. Narrative prose is about people, the extraordinary situations they find themselves in, the implications of those situations, and how they get out of them.

It is common to think of writing as being fact or fiction, but what makes storywriting so important for children is the broad dimensions of thought it is capable of embracing. Novelists can spend more time researching historical or scientific information than writing the novel for which it is intended. A child writing a story about a family vacationing abroad first needs to find out about passports and visas; preventive medicines; travel routes, climatic conditions, and terrain; foreign languages; and local history, currency, customs, food, sports, and pastimes.

Because storytelling stimulates multidimensional thought and allows students to select and use knowledge drawn from the whole curriculum (and from other areas of human experience such as mores, philosophy, and psychology), it occupies a unique place in the teaching of writing.

Storytelling once dominated the fine arts. The experimental ambience of the twentieth century has tended to overshadow art as narrative, although there has been a reemergence of figurative storytelling of late. Pictorial composition, once popular in the classroom, took a nosedive in the sixties and was replaced by mixed-media explorations and archetypal

"Coke can" art. That spirit still lingers, but there are signs that narrative pictures are making a comeback in our classrooms.

Illustration, once regarded as a decorative appendage to children's books, has in recent years been elevated to the status of text. It is now common for educators to refer to children's "reading" the pictures in their storybooks and finding in them a parallel story rivaling the written one. Illustration, as much an intellectual process as writing is, requires children to research their material and to think and feel with an artist's eye. Information gathering permeates both forms; but when the two coexist, a new and vital dimension is added to the creative experience. Children learning to interrelate these two "languages" acquire inimitable insight into communication.

Picture Books, Illustrated Books, Books with Illustrations

The concept behind a storybook determines the kinds of illustrations it holds (if any) and how many there are. The general pattern is this: the younger the child the book is intended for, the more illustrations there are and the closer they are intertwined with the text. As children grow older, illustrations tend to play a more supportive role and there are fewer of them. By the time children reach adolescence, and we use the word *novel* or *fiction* rather than *story* to describe their reading, illustrations almost disappear.

Why this happens has to do partly with the way children are conditioned by how we, as educators, think reading should progress—a greater emphasis on learning through words at the expense of pictures—and partly with the changes children experience as they mature into adults and become engrossed in specific categories of decoding.

In the *picture book*, words and pictures cohabit the page and are narratively interrelated. For the very young, each sentence has a corresponding illustration. Sometimes pictures take over the page completely.

Illustrated books emphasize the words; the illustrations play a secondary although still important role. Here the illustrator's craft is used to emphasize or enlarge some point in the text.

Stories for the older child invariably have just a handful of line drawings; these are *books with illustrations*. The writer and illustrator in this category are detached, the illustrator selecting a few highlights from the text for visual treatment.

Students' responses to implementing writing and illustration projects loosely reflect these categories. Some children naturally lean more toward writing, so in their work there is an imbalance of writing to illustration;

pupils who are "good at art" tend to concentrate on illustrations, perhaps at the cost of their writing development.

Some communication tasks can be more successfully accomplished through art than through words. And in some circumstances, illustrating is a wholly inappropriate addition to the writing process. Only by knowing the scope and uses of illustration can one decide when and where it will cohabit successfully—and purposefully—with words.

Making Pictures

Many teachers and parents shy away from teaching children to draw—and particularly to illustrate—because they feel they lack the necessary skills. This book attempts to show how non–art specialists and parents can ease children into the art of narrative visual expression.

Making Basic Books

Children writing their own books has become a central idea in my educational philosophy. Discovering basic origami book forms in the mid-eighties opened a door for me into children's writing that I had not imagined possible. These beautiful books are incredibly easy to make. All you need is a sheet of paper, a pair of scissors, and simple folding, cutting, and refolding techniques. (The appendix contains instructions for how to make basic concertina and origami books.)

In this book I deal with illustrated narratives primarily in the context of these basic book forms. I have written elsewhere (1990, 1993) about the many approaches to the book arts in education and about other kinds of books (pop-up and movable books, for example) that can be made simply from single sheets of paper. (Hardcover binding and Japanese side binding, which I touch on here, I describe in detail in *A Book of One's Own*. For more traditional approaches to craft bookbinding in schools, Pauline Johnson's *Creative Bookbinding* is an excellent primer.)

Publishing Children's Illustrated Books

Because basic books are constructed from single sheets of paper that can be opened out flat, they can be easily photocopied. The implications are enormous: a child's book can be published in any quantity and circulated in and outside the school. And via the computer and the electronic super-highway, the concept of a school-based community of writers takes on global proportions.

Since children acquire the language of illustration by learning to draw, to structure pictorial compositions, and to relate to a text in a special way, my attention here is directed to the formative aspects of narrative illustration rather than its craft; strategies for working with color and printmaking techniques are therefore largely omitted.

Analyzing professional book illustrations takes us part of the way toward understanding how to create them ourselves, but doing so exposes us to the danger that we will copy techniques without digesting the underlying truth of their structure. That is something we must discover for ourselves.

We must also be aware that making pictures is different from writing. It can take a professional artist six months or more to provide illustrations for a book that has been only a few days in the writing. Similarly, a child can spend a whole morning providing an illustration for a one-sentence episode, can spend as much time on making a rough sketch for an illustration as on the final picture. How much time to afford each writing/drawing task is a question unique to the book arts in the classroom, one that requires the teacher's judgment and discretion.

Most of the examples in this book are the work of children from schools in the urban communities of Greater Manchester, where I live, teach, conduct my research, and have my art studio. Many of these children come from deprived backgrounds and/or have learning difficulties or motivational problems, and making books has been a way for dedicated teachers to raise the self-esteem of the school community. I would need to profile the individuals whose work is shown here in order to convey the true extent of their achievement. Readers must accept that only a part of their story is told.

Finally, while students need a goal to aim for, teachers must be realistic about what they can achieve; the temptation to base this book around above-average students' work has therefore been avoided.

1

Making Storybooks in Preschool and Kindergarten

BOOKS AND THE EMERGENT AUTHOR

We now know for certain that the children who handle books confidently before they go to school, and have enjoyed being read to, are those who learn to read in school with the most success.   —MARGARET MEEK

Building an Enthusiasm for Books

"As a child I was taught that books are very precious things that must be treated accordingly," says teacher Michelle Haydock. "A trip to the library was a highlight of the week, to be allowed to choose a special book to take home for seven whole days! I was therefore distressed to find that the children at the nursery school in which I work didn't seem to share my respect for books. The interest in books and storytelling was there, but the way in which books were treated was upsetting, with frequent torn pages, or books left lying on the floor. So how could I develop this interest in stories and books and also foster an attitude of respect?"

Because she was involved with the United Kingdom's National Oracy Project, Michelle wanted to find an approach to oracy that reflected her love of books. Books entertain, comfort, stimulate, help children understand newly felt emotions, and create a very special relationship between adult and child.

Michelle's students had always been free to go into the book corner when they wished, but it was often the last choice: the other areas were more appealing. Because the children had recently become interested in monsters, Michelle decided to incorporate this interest into a new look for the book corner. She displayed pictures of imaginary and real animals, together with books such as *Where the Wild Things Are*, by Maurice Sendak, and David McKee's *Not Now, Bernard*.

As Michelle read *Where the Wild Things Are* aloud to her students, even the "fidgeters" were still, their faces rapt with anticipation. The story quickly became a favorite. Michelle created a "wild thing" puppet, and this stimulated a variety of language work. Children told the story confidently to each other, embellishing it with episodes of their own devising.

The transition from storytelling to book art came naturally. "When I suggested to the children that we should make our own wild-things books, they responded enthusiastically," says Michelle. "The basic origami book seemed a good starting point for children so young. They helped make the creases, and one or two were even able to control a pair of scissors."

It was amazing how the children were able to order their thoughts to fit the book format. They had a grasp of sequencing and put the character of Max on the first page. When invited to choose a title for their book, most suggested the Sendak one, but Stephanie, almost four years old, invented her own: *The Wild Things Will Eat You Up!* Every child finished his or her book, which was quite an achievement, especially for the ones who had learning difficulties.

With enthusiasm for the Sendak characters still alive the following week, Michelle decided to have the whole class make a pop-up book. The activity progressed from making pop-up constructions of a forest and a boat to acting out the story to using a music synthesizer to make wild-thing noises.

The students' newfound enthusiasm for books they could make themselves took a new direction the following week, when they visited a bookshop. Michelle bought a copy of *The Jolly Postman*, by Janet and Allan Ahlberg, and on returning to school spent several days opening the envelopes inside the book and revealing the missives inside them. Inevitably, the children wanted to make postmen and postwomen books. (I describe this book form in detail in *Books Searching for Authors*.) It took two sessions, one in which to write the letters and address the envelopes, the other to compose the text and create the illustrations.

During these weeks of working with the book arts, the children's drawings became more informed and their oral exchanges more fluent. They asked questions about "book stuff," like putting the author's name on the front cover and a bar code on the back, because they were actively dealing with these things.

The students also became more relaxed when collaborating with one another, something very evident in their production of *Our Easter Book*, the centerpiece of the school's special Easter display.

"I was eager that the book arts should be seen as a way of recording and identifying experience," remarks Michelle. "Our Under the Sea theme in artwork and performance was photographed and bound using hard covers." The students helped put their work into the book and typed the identifying labels into the computer, which Michelle then printed. A different page from the book was displayed each day of the Easter season. The pride the children experienced from having their work on view was evident, and they reminded Michelle when she forgot to turn a page.

Part of the sea project also involved making a concertina book. The advantage of this form is that all the pages can be seen at once, like a long mural. The students used all kinds of techniques in their concertina book—bubble printing, marbling, string painting.

The final book in this literacy segment was the most ambitious. First, the class brainstormed a theme, one that (no surprise) featured familiar storybook characters—pigs and monkeys—combined with real-life experiences like being naughty, being sent to bed, and crying when hurt. Then they drafted the story on large sheets of paper:

> *One day the little pig set off to go to the fair. On the way he picked some turnips.*
>
> *The little boy saw him and said, "No!" He sent the pig away.*
>
> *The monkey came and got the turnip off the little pig and said, "Don't you pick my turnips. You are naughty. Go to bed!"*
>
> *The naughty pig was sent to bed. The little boy and the monkey went to the fair without the pig.*
>
> *All the children were at the fair.*

After the planning phase was completed, each child chose a part of the story to illustrate on large sheets of paper, which were then glued into a ready-made side-bound book. (Side binding is perfect for a book that may have to grow to almost any size. You simply collate the pages and then stitch them together down the edge of the spine instead of through the folds as in conventional saddle-stitched binding.) Stephanie felt especially proud at being able to sew the large pages together along the edges.

Michelle printed the story out on the computer and pasted the appropriate text opposite the relevant illustration. The children then took the completed book around to other classes and read it aloud. (Two two-page spreads from the book are shown in Figure 1–1.)

Michelle believes these book projects benefited her students in a number of ways:

- They acquired greater self-confidence and self-esteem.
- They saw themselves as real storytellers.

FIGURE 1–1. Two two-page spreads from *The Little Boy, the Pig, and the Monkey.*

The naughty pig was sent
to bed. The little boy and
the monkey went to the
fair without the pig.

The monkey came and got
the turnip off the little pig
and said,
"Don't you pick my turnips.
You are naughty. Go to bed!"

- They were able to take pride in the work they produced.
- They acquired independence by creating their own versions of known stories.
- They improved their language fluency.
- They improved their interpersonal skills.
- They were introduced to verbally demanding situations.
- They became familiar with book vocabulary.
- They developed their intellectual skills by integrating picture making and language.
- They learned how to structure and plan a book.
- They developed fine motor skills: folding paper; threading a needle; sewing; and manipulating scissors, pens, crayons, and paintbrushes.

Michelle concludes, "The book arts made [the school staff] as a team examine our own practice and the provisions we made for pupils. It encouraged the very best work from children and enabled all the staff to see them in a new light. These tasks necessitated new ways of using emerging skills and acquiring techniques."

Using the Book Arts to Teach Literacy

Vanessa Kershaw also teaches in a preschool. Like Michelle, she has found the book form an effective way to teach literacy. She makes the point that it is too easy for children to believe that books have some kind of mystical existence or that they're the products of bookstores.

"When I began introducing the book arts to the pupils I found I was still learning a lot myself," says Vanessa. "I let them play freely with the basic books from one sheet of paper that I had made, so that they could familiarize themselves with them. Up until that point we had been using plain sheets of paper in the writing corner. In the second half of the term, I felt more confident with the book arts, and so I set out with a number of objectives in mind."

These were:

- To ensure that children were familiar with the way books worked and the special terminology involved.
- To help children become independent and imaginative book artists and to enjoy making books.
- To develop students' ability to work in groups.
- To concentrate on the development of emergent literacy.

Vanessa began by using simple concertina books made from several sizes and qualities of paper; she put them in the writing corner with the usual sheets of lined and unlined paper to test the children's reaction.

"As they discovered the books, they came to me and asked about them," says Vanessa. "All day the corner was well populated and a lot of activity went on in connection with those books. Looking back, this kind of reaction is typical of all the book-art work I've done. Children find it extremely exciting and stimulating; it attracts those who don't usually enjoy making marks on paper."

At first Vanessa intervened very little. She allowed the children to explore the books and use them as they wished. Some children stretched out the concertina so they could write across its whole length; others turned the pages. It was interesting to observe students who handled the pieces of folded paper *as a book* and/or distinguished "writing"—as named marks—from pictures.

James, three years nine months, was mainly interested in playing with sand and water, although he would sit in the story corner and look at the books there. His favorite story was about a little red hen, and he chose this as the subject of his own storybook—the first time he had attempted anything of this sort. The cover had a picture of the red hen and the seven remaining pages consisted of his "writing" (see Figure 1–2).

The next week Vanessa brought some lift-the-flap books (like *Where's Spot?* by Eric Hill) to the writing table, hoping to spur the children to creative action. One of the first students to plunge in was Clare, who wanted to make a *Little Miss Muffett* book. Vanessa gave her a simple folding

FIGURE 1–2. Two pages from James's *The Little Red Hen.*

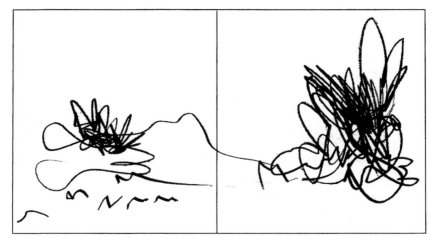

book, and Clare drew Miss Muffett on the cover. After that, Vanessa asked Clare what she wanted each page to say and wrote the words down as Clare dictated. Clare didn't want to use the whole rhyme, just extracts, and was adamant that there should be a flap on the back page for the spider to pounce out from.

Some of the children found the concertina books difficult to use. They unfolded the sheet of paper and laid it out flat because they couldn't manipulate it easily. To overcome this problem Vanessa began making triangular-shaped books from large sheets of paper. (I describe this book form in detail in *A Book of One's Own*.) Seeing their own special book being made right in front of them made it all the more important and personal to them, and the pointed corners were certainly more easy to turn than the rectangular concertina form.

Each term Vanessa's preschool routinely gives its teachers an album in which to keep a photographic record of the class, but Vanessa decided that this time she would make the album herself (a hardcover concertina book) and decorate it with her own marbled papers. She asked the students to draw their own portraits for the album, thus making a book that was unique in every way (see Figure 1–3). The hard binding and the carefully mounted and presented work inside increased the children's respect for "homemade" books and showed them their own work could look as good as that of any published book.

In the second half of the term, Vanessa thought it seemed right to introduce the concept of a book systematically. During story time, she talked about the parts of a book, like the *spine* and the *cover*, and the difference between *portrait* and *landscape* orientation. As Vanessa's own knowledge of the book form increased, she also began to talk about *layouts*, *borders*,

FIGURE 1–3. Vanessa's "photograph album," opened out to its full length and displayed in the school hall.

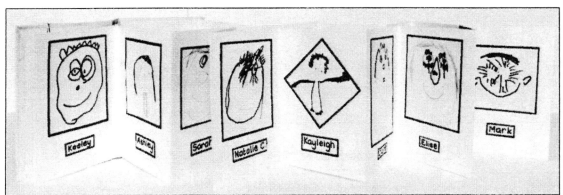

doors, *flaps*, and *pop-ups*, and visited libraries and bookstores to find
books that exemplified these techniques.

Up until this point, the book form had suggested the story to go inside
it. Now Vanessa wanted to start with an idea and then find a form to match.
The class theme at the time was wild animals, and she asked her students

FIGURE 1–4. Two two-page spreads from *Leo the Lion*.

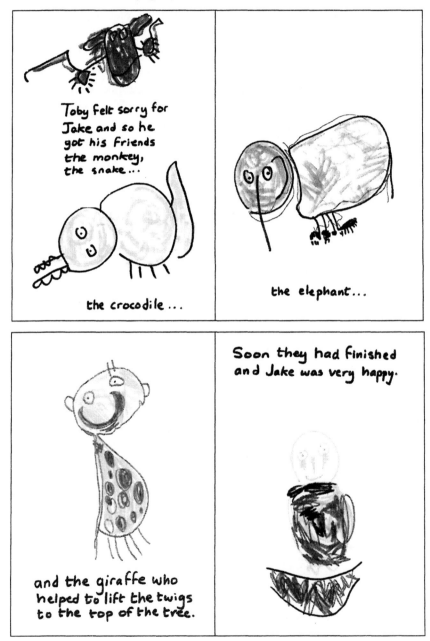

for ideas. Somebody suggested a lion hiding in the jungle, so the class talked about how animals hide themselves.

Vanessa then remembered *Peepo!* by Janet and Allan Ahlberg, a book in which the reader looks through holes cut in the page. Using a similar technique, she made some simple single-fold cards. The children drew an animal on one half and cut out a free-form design on the other; the cutout half acted as camouflage when pressed on top of the drawing. When everyone had finished, Vanessa used the cards to play animal-identification games with the children.

Next Vanessa tried using a puppet to stimulate story narratives, from which the students would develop a plot storyboard and then a book. She decided to work with a smaller group, ten pupils in all. This project was also linked to the wild animal theme. To prepare the students, she read them *Have You Seen the Crocodile?* and *Not Me, Said the Monkey*, both by Colin West.

Vanessa brought a lion puppet to the next story time. Th pupils improvised a lion character named Toby, and ideas about things that could happen to him came quite readily. Vanessa wrote the story down on large sheets of paper, using the children's words and adding a few linking words when necessary. Then she read the story back to the students, and they made some changes and corrections.

When the draft was finished, the students planned the book one page at a time. Vanessa read a sentence (or part of a sentence) and asked how it could be illustrated. The pupils then decided which parts of the story they wanted to tell with pictures. Two children helped Vanessa dye a large sheet of paper to be the cover lining, and Vanessa bound the finished book along the side. (Two spreads are shown in Figure 1–4.)

"Looking back over this book period it was with a sense of achievement that I could identify how the pupils were gaining experience at making a number of different kinds of books," says Vanessa. "I was also able to assess how 'book literate' they had become."

This experiment in making books really whetted Vanessa's appetite. "I want to make illustration an important part of the development of mark-making skills, and to widen the writing inquiry to nonfiction—investigation, for example. This work has clearly shown me the advantages of using the book art approach."

2

Toward a
Finished Picture Book

THE NASCENT AUTHOR AND ILLUSTRATOR

If it is the experience of authorship which helps authors develop, then it follows that children should, from the start, be given opportunities to explore what it means to be an author. —NIGEL HALL

Figure 2–1 is a two-page spread from six-year-old Tim's commercial exercise book. It's a typical presentation—a page or so of writing along with an illustration. At first glance, it seems Tim is writing reasonably well for his age. But like so many children at this stage of development, he is having difficulty with two major writing components: conceiving sentences and shaping a plot.

Meandering sentences, often starting with the pronoun *he*, together with an implausible plot (the main character is murdered but then is taken to the hospital with a broken leg), show that Tim is not thinking very clearly. There is a kind of beginning, middle, and end, but the structure is weak (Fred's brother is introduced but has no role to play). The illustration of flowerlike trees throws no light on the plot and adds no new information about the setting.

Contemporaneously with this exercise book entry, as part of a special book project, Tim created the eight-page concertina book in Figure 2–2. In a concertina book, one page is reserved as the title page, another (in effect the back page) for "back-page copy"—a plot synopsis, information about the author, publisher's logo. This leaves six single pages for the contents of the book: four uninterrupted pages (two spreads) on the front, and two (one spread) on the back. (See the appendix for instructions.)

With assistance, some six-year-olds can make this simple book themselves, but as this book project was limited to just four one-hour-and-fifteen-minute sessions, each member of the group was given a ready-made book.

Getting Acquainted

It is one of the mysteries of the book form that when a piece of folded paper is described as a book it instantly becomes a cultural artifact. The group members spent the first few minutes of the introductory session handling their concertina books and finding their way through them. First their teacher, Judith, took them on a guided tour: "On this side, there are four pages for our story. Let's count them—one, two, three, four. And on the other side there are two more pages for our story. The other two pages will be used for the cover, and for saying something about ourselves. We will do that when we have finished writing our book."

Then Judith described the plan: left-side pages for writing, right-side

FIGURE 2–1. A two-page spread from Tim's commercial exercise book.

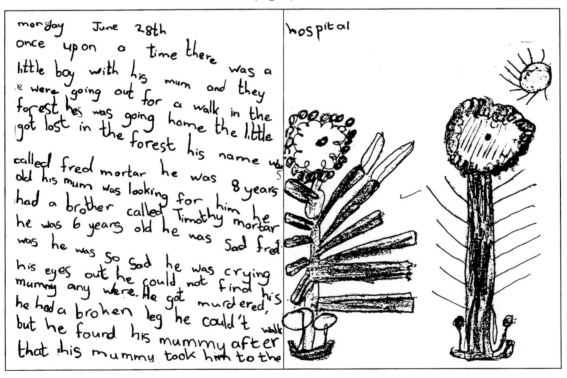

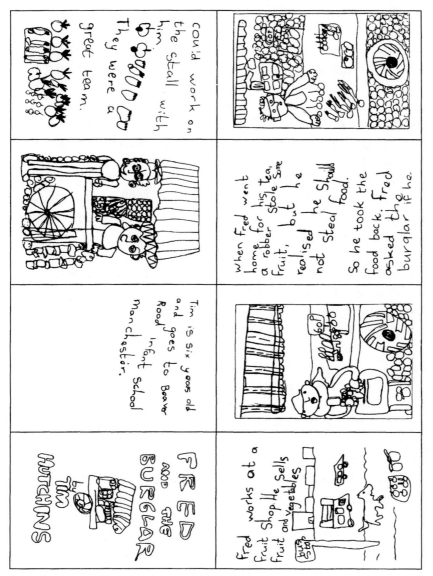

FIGURE 2–2. Tim's concertina book, *Fred and the Burglar.*

pages for illustrations, in effect restructuring the six story pages into three linked double-page spreads—three watertight compartments from which these authors could not deviate. They could not write and illustrate more than three alternating pages, because there was nowhere for these additional words and pictures to go, and to write or illustrate less than three would leave "holes" in the book. This designated layout turns the pages into symbolic icons, reserved for something very special indeed. It makes children think in a page way, a very disciplined way, which marshals and refines words like nothing else can.

Can You Picture It?

Judith then told the group to do the whole book, including the illustrations, in pencil. When drawing, children naturally want to use color, either pencil crayons or felt-tip pens. Both instruments have their uses, very significant uses at that, but using them tends to be very time-consuming. Devoting too much time to the illustrations means less time for the writing. And spending too long on the project as a whole can kill creativity in children this young, and it is difficult to reverse their loss of interest.

(Some practical advice here. It's important to have a supply of spare paper cut to the appropriate "page" size. Children, like adults, so easily become dissatisfied with their work and need to be able to redraw and/or rewrite on these rectangles of paper, which can then be glued down over the unacceptable pages.)

The Market, by Rosemary Lowndes and Claude Kailer, consists of a foldout market stall and pressout cards depicting four market traders and their produce. Judith deployed one of the tradesmen in the stall and placed the three-dimensional display so that the whole group could see it clearly, using it as a starting point for both the theme of the story and the first illustration.

Who was the man standing in the market? What was he selling? Judith asked the children to give the tradesman a name, so that even before a plot emerged, they had established the embryo of a character. Their task now was to draw the scene before them.

Children can "say" as much in a drawing as they can in a written or spoken story, but at this stage of development they have problems identifying and manipulating two-dimensional space, just as they have problems dealing with time and space in narrative. We are ready to help young students manipulate concepts like *today*, *tomorrow*, *that evening*, *over there*, *the next town*. But we are less aware that they also need help coming to terms with that other great panoramic zone, the picture plane. The visual status of a centrally placed object is subject to the influence of the other objects around it. (This idea is discussed in more detail in Chapter 5.) Take just one of the supporting objects away, and the composition falls apart, the "meaning" lost.

A pictorial scene can house an infinite number of objects, all of which the onlooker reacts to in different ways as his or her imagination tries to make sense of them in the context of a self-determined story. So where do artists get their images?

One way is to "collect ideas" in a sketchbook, but taking thirty six-year-olds out to draw a market scene has organizational problems to say

FIGURE 2–3. An example of "curling up in the corner of the page."

FIGURE 2–4. Helping students plan object in space.

the least! Secondary sources of imagery, like magazine illustrations, are always less viable substitutes, and purists frown on their use (though in the context of children's illustrating they have their uses). The compromise solution is to use a mixture of approaches, combining drawing from life with more accessible references, just as children's writing combines their own invented ideas with ideas gleaned from stories they know.

Using a three-dimensional book as a visual reference lies somewhere between a primary and secondary source of information. The artwork is secondary, but since it stands as a piece of paper sculpture with 360-degree viewpoints, it can be drawn in the same way as three-dimensional objects.

When children are told to "draw a picture" they invariably bypass the frightening prospect of the entire picture plane and instead "curl up in a corner of the page" (see Figure 2–3). This corner is a safety zone, because it denies the spatial territory of the page. It is a place to hide in, not a place to work in.

There is a way to head off this spatial cop-out. In the first illustration area of each student's book, the structure of the stall was outlined very lightly in a dominant, central position (see Figure 2–4), thus creating a spatial field the students could relate to and work from. To have outlined an abstract arrangement of shapes (see Figure 2–5) would have given them the same framework in which to place their ideas, but young children really need clearly recognizable images.

Providing more than just the base plan would have been dangerously

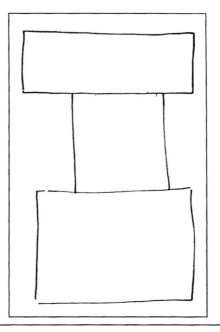

FIGURE 2–5. Abstract shapes provide a framework but without recognizable images.

near to becoming a *fait accompli* coloring book, in which the picture is already made. One has to provide just enough of a structure for children to have the confidence to "go in there" and make it their own.

Just as we discuss with children not only what they write but how they write, so we need to draw out of them the composition of a picture as well as how to draw it. "Talking through" pictorial ideas is the backbone of much art classroom practice. But there must also be room to accelerate the visualizing process in certain circumstances. Writing teachers have any number of strategies for giving children a structural framework within which narratives can be invented and reviewed. The picture-making aid just described does this from a visual stance.

And it is interesting that in both Tim's stall illustration in Figure 2–2 and the stall illustrations of another group member, Matthew (see Figure 2–6), the skeletal drawing has not been rigidly adhered to. Wheel proportions, canopy shape, and distances between the parts of the stall vary considerably. In fact, each of Matthew's illustrations is an improvement on the one before. The base plan is like a musical theme around which a composition is woven. Without the melody there is no subject for the music.

Tim's drawing of Fred (a reappearance of the character in Tim's exercise book story?) in an environment that establishes his identity cements a narrative plot structure. It is a simple, logical step for Tim to start his story with "Fred works at a fruit shop. He sells fruit and vegetables."

FIGURE 2–6. Matthew's stall illustration.

The Middle Section–Where It All Happens

The halfway point in these three-section books tends to be where the action is. If a character is satisfactorily introduced in the first section, and a situation is resolved in the third section, then there must be a degree of tension in the middle that needs to be resolved.

This is where children often get lost in a maze of directionless plots and subplots, as Tim did in his exercise book story. But because all the action must be tailored to this small space, smaller than a postcard, the book form comes to the rescue. Everything must be reduced to clearly stated events.

Tim's first oral draft for the middle section was, "Fred went home to have his tea and then he went to bed"—not a very gripping story, and there was still another page to go. How could the story be made more interesting? Could a new character be introduced? Aha, a robber. This became, "A robber stole some fruit and ran away."

There were now two undeveloped story strands: Fred at home asleep, and a robber who had disappeared. Tim had to find some way to integrate the two characters and to resolve the moral dilemma of theft. After a few perambulations none of which provided a satisfactory resolution to the story, the idea of repentance emerged—the robber returns the produce to the stall.

The story now set, Tim was able to turn his attention to the second illustration. Its basic structure is the same as the first (the fruit stall), but here the character of the robber is placed not at the front of the stall as Fred was, but at the back. This may seem a minor distinction, but it is significant.

In the first illustration, Fred commands a strategic position, center left. He is clearly established here as boss. The robber, on the other hand, presumably steals from behind the stall so that he will not be noticed, and so logically returns the stolen goods in the same manner. He is further back, in the middle ground of the picture, a repentant figure, but still a shadowy one. The spatial dynamics of the page have defined this symbolic status and the relationship between the two characters. (Notice how much better drawn the vegetables are here than in the first illustration.) Tim then penned the narrative in the verso page.

Every End a New Beginning

Finding a satisfactory end to his story was the hardest part of the whole task for Tim. At first he suggested that Fred could call the police, but he couldn't feel his way from this to some kind of fulfillment, for either Fred or the repentant robber. Then he thought they might go off on vacation together to Disneyland, but on reflection he conceded that Fred was unlikely to make so extroverted an offer, especially to someone who had stolen from him. A more gentle, domestic conclusion was needed. Other children in the group joined in here, and the final version emerged: "Fred asked the burglar if he could work on the stall with him. They were a great team."

The final illustration was modeled on the same plan as the other two. Tim was getting bored with redrawing fruit and vegetables by now. (This is one of the drawbacks of illustrating stories with a narrow setting. Later he will learn from professional book illustrators how a story set in one location can be visually resourceful and repeat nothing.) The second drawing was an improvement on the first, but the last one shows weariness beginning to set in.

What is significant is the placing and size of the two actors. Both are now at the front of the stall and stand at either side of it as symbolically equal partners. Fred, based on *The Market* figure, is seen wearing hat, neckerchief, and long apron, but the ex-thief is a less defined figure and the black ring around his eyes isolates him. After Tim finished the drawing, he wrote in the text, starting the final episode on the bottom of the middle text page.

Finishing Off

The last textual stage was "back-page" autobiographical details: "One sentence about me." In this case, Tim also asked if he could draw in the spaces around the text. This is understandable. The middle section full of

FIGURE 2–7. Tim's first attempt at a cover design.

words makes the first and last textual pages appear half empty. Tim drew an effective street scene under the first page of text and fruit and vegetables on the final text page.

To complete the book, Tim then tackled the cover. (This is one of the last tasks of professional book designers, so it is fitting it should be the last task when children make their own books.) Tim's first attempt at designing a cover (Figure 2–7) shows just how essential design education is to graphic communication. Judith then showed the children how to "draw" the cover words rather than write them and to leave space for an illustration. There are numerous strategies for arranging words and images on a book cover, but to keep it simple Judith used the following formula: title, top; picture, middle; author's name, bottom.

Another Example

There is much more that could be said about Tim's book and what he has learned about defining and communicating through language, but let's move on to look at the work of Matthew, another student in this group.

Figure 2–8 is a writing exercise Matthew produced during the same time the book-art sessions were being held. It is clear and sequentially structured for a pupil of his age (six years four months), but it is also dull. It's hard to believe Matthew felt any real commitment to it. The illustration offers lighthearted relief from the writing, shows that Matthew has been seduced by color and shape, but it is not a visual partner to the linguistic statement.

Matthew created his first concertina book, *John's Adventure* (see Figure 2–9), using the same process Tim and the others did. He profited from the same guidelines relative to the broad structure of illusionary space, but he seemed better able to improvise his way through the imagery and onto the page. He formulated his story with greater ease; it was as if he had been waiting to discover this book form.

His second book, *Elma and the Toy Soldier* (see Figure 2–10), was inspired by *The Magic Toyshop*, a three-dimensional storybook by Michael Welply that opens up to display toys on shelves. (The photograph at the beginning of this chapter shows pupils using this book as a reference as they work on their own books.)

There is no mistaking Matthew's progress in just two days of book art. The first page of *John's Adventure* is prosaic, offering no hint of the excitement to come, while the first page of *Elma* draws the reader in immediately. The middle development section in the second book contains three episodes, versus one in the first book. The ending of the latter is more rounded, more engaging, and more involved than the former.

FIGURE 2–8. Matthew's writing exercise.

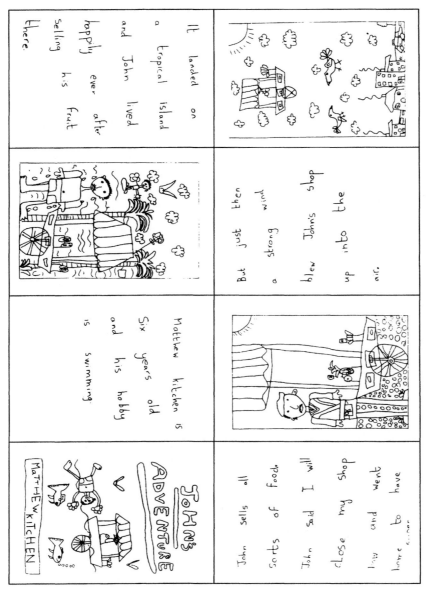

FIGURE 2–9. Matthew's first concertina book.

In both books the interrelationship between text and illustration grows harmoniously. The first illustration of *John's Adventure* has no background other than a schematic sun; the last one shows John perspiring in tropical heat, and a surfer and hang glider provide interest in the top third of the illustration.

The second illustration in *Elma* depicts Elma and the toy soldier skating, with a middle-ground audience of onlookers. The top curved decoration of the stadium echoes the curve of the ice rink lower down. The artistry of words and visual images makes a total aesthetic experience. The

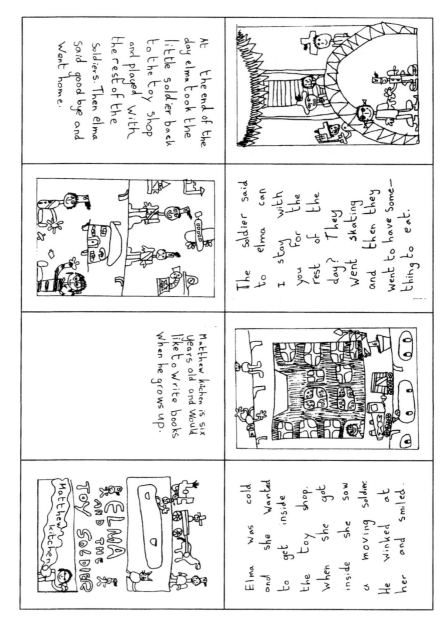

FIGURE 2–10. Matthew's second concertina book.

words do some of the telling, and the pictures tell a story independent of the text yet inextricably tied to it.

Seeing Is Believing

While written narratives are records of what *has* happened, illustrations are always perceived in the eternal present. When we look at an illustration of a man climbing over a wall, it is happening now, just as the moving images in TV and film are always happening now. That is why it helps the emergent writer to create a visual image for a plot situation: drawings keep still and don't go away as the ephemeral images of the imagination do, even when they have been articulated verbally.

What the book does, even in its most basic form like the concertina, is to make the weaving of ideas possible. It stays perfectly still while words and pictures grow in and through it. In the end children have before them an object endowed with all the power that the book as an institution has to give it. It is a transforming experience.

Every Book Stimulates the Next One

Timing a book-making project requires fine-tuning. Too much time on one aspect or another at the expense of the overall shape, and the thing easily falls apart; the book will remain unfinished. If children feel the flush of success, they will be more likely to aim higher in their next piece of work. What children achieve in writing and graphic communication has as much to do with awareness as with ability. The book form makes them look again and so think again. The exercise book never does that.

One must always look behind words and see what is underneath. Refined writing and drawing exist on the edge of the child's cognition, waiting to be embraced.

After their book experience, these children went back to writing in exercise books. With the book form no longer there to uplift them, their commitment to writing and visual communication deteriorated. Reinforcement and encouragement is a continual process. Children slip back into bad ways with astonishing ease. Teachers must insist on quality on every page of a book, as if it were a work of art—as indeed it is.

3

From Storyboard to Book

SKETCHING, DRAFTING, MAKING, AND PRESENTING

When art becomes truly integrated throughout every stage of the writing process, both children's creative processes and their finished products share a quality of richness previously unequaled.   —BETH OLSHANSKY

This chapter profiles a book-making project I conducted with a group of "more able" and "less able" children, whose writing and conceptualizing skills varied greatly. I used computer-designed storyboard plans in which the penned narrative derives much of its structure from the drawn images. I anticipated that this highly structured approach to writing and graphic communication would strengthen narrative sequencing. (Then too, laying out a book in this way is not that far removed from the techniques used by professional writer/illustrators.)

Picturing the Story

The six storyboard boxes in Figure 3–1 correspond to the six single pages of the basic origami book (see the appendix). (They are numbered according to standard publishing procedure—verso pages even, recto pages odd—so the story starts on page 2.) The narrative structure prescribed for each of the boxes follows a familiar cyclical pattern: a charac-

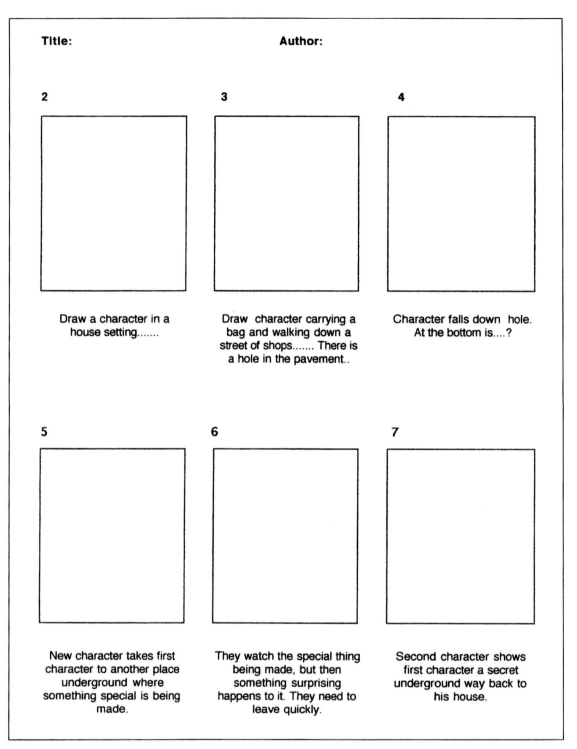

FIGURE 3–1. A planned storyboard.

ter leaves his or her home, goes on an adventure, has an encounter and an ordeal, but returns home safely at the end.

The character is established but not defined. He or she starts at home (page 2), but then goes out shopping (page 3). The character falls down a hole in the sidewalk (page 4), at which point the student must decide what is at the bottom of the hole. A new character is introduced who takes the first character to a place where an unspecified "something special" is being made (page 5). A surprising development (also unspecified) occurs in this new location (page 6). Finally, a way of resolving and concluding the story is implied (page 7).

I distributed this sheet to the group, and we discussed it together. The students brainstormed an initial character—age, sex, and occupation—then briefly described this character to their partner before sketching in the pictorial narrative box by box.

The first two environments (pages 2 and 3) present no major problems, as the plot here is prescriptive. But on page 4 the student has to devise the plot development ("At the bottom [of the hole] is. . . ?") The introduction of a second character on page 5 involves inventing (a) an identity and (b) a location. This character is less developed than the first and plays a facilitating role.

At this point the intervention of an object (perhaps a machine) must grasp the reader's attention. This offsetting of the animate against the inanimate is a classical dynamic of storywriting. Inevitably a new forward thrust comes when something unexpected happens (page 6), and an escape route (another archetypal device) must be found to return the main character home safe and sound (page 7).

As in the cinema, movement and transition is speeded up in picture stories. Only main developments are defined. The fact that the main character moves effortlessly from page 4 to page 5 implies that the fall through the hole has not been physically damaging. The transition between the machine episode (page 5) and the "surprising" plot development (page 6) takes place in the invisible chamber of time between boxes. These things need not be questioned: factual details like this are swallowed up by the swiftness of the action.

The students had already seen the origami books they would later be working in, and knew that the six parts of the plot mirrored the book's form. At this stage there had been no workshops in the techniques of drawing figures in movement, settings, or space. I simply told them to "draw the story."

James (age six) created a robust and confident visual narrative (Figure 3–2). He draws the second character from the side, thus implying movement (although the main character remains front view throughout), and the individual traits of the characters are consistent. (Because all six boxes are on the same sheet, you can instantly compare one box with another.)

Title: **Author:**

2

Draw a character in a
house setting.......

3

Draw character carrying a
bag and walking down a
street of shops....... There is
a hole in the pavement..

4

Character falls down hole.
At the bottom is....?

5

New character takes first
character to another place
underground where
something special is being
made.

6

They watch the special thing
being made, but then
something surprising
happens to it. They need to
leave quickly.

7

Second character shows
first character a secret
underground way back to
his house.

FIGURE 3–2. James's completed storyboard.

Aarash is two years older than James. His drawings (see Figure 3–3) reveal more information about the characters. There is greater spatial awareness; environments indicate their location or function in more detail. All but one of Aarash's figures are side views, although the first one is nondynamic and stationary. The final yes-I'm-happily-back-home pose shows he has an instinct for visual communication. The passive scene setting of the beginning and the equally inactive resolution anchor the suspense that lies between them.

In her storyboard (Figure 3–4), Katherine, age ten, demonstrates an elementary knowledge of picture sequencing. She instinctively introduces her character in a front view before using side views in the action boxes. On page 5, Katherine correctly indicates a conversation by having the characters face each other; she also differentiates their sex via dress and hairstyle. Figures are drawn well down the foreground area (compare this with James's boxes, where the figures stand firmly on the base line). Finally, Katherine has the visual intelligence to draw the details of the kitchen scene on page 7 precisely the same as that on page 2.

Writing the Story

The six text boxes in Figure 3–5 correspond to the six picture boxes. The students, aided by the printed suggestions, first orally summarized the story, then wrote down the narrative. (The small boxes necessitate brief episodes—a useful visual device for concentrating the mind!) No one was allowed to start with "Once upon a time . . ."—alternative beginnings were brainstormed.

James's, Aarash's, and Katherine's drafts (Figures 3–6, 3–7, and 3–8) show how much the graphic segregation of narrative episodes assists the refining process. The children write with a degree of confidence, although they make common mistakes. Errors and necessary changes are recognized more easily because one sees the linear progression of what is happening in the pictures. All in all, the programmed episodes, in connection with step-by-step collaborative editing, have produced a tighter, clearer story than a child would be likely to produce working on a conventional notepad.

The hardest task was structuring an ending. Most students found it hard to come up with a way for the main character to journey from underground back to his or her house. Even when a way was finally found, the endings lacked a well-rounded cadence; they were a passive rather than an active finale.

Creating the Book

Finally the students transformed their sketches and narrative drafts into a finished book using a page-layout template (Figure 3–9) showing the

FIGURE 3–3. Aarash's completed storyboard.

Title: **Author:**

2

Draw a character in a
house setting.......

3

Draw character carrying a
bag and walking down a
street of shops....... There is
a hole in the pavement.

4

Character falls down hole.
At the bottom is....?

5

New character takes first
character to another place
underground where
something special is being
made.

6

They watch the special thing
being made, but then
something surprising
happens to it. They need to
leave quickly.

7

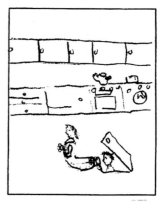

Second character shows
first character a secret
underground way back to
his house.

FIGURE 3–4. Katherine's completed storyboard.

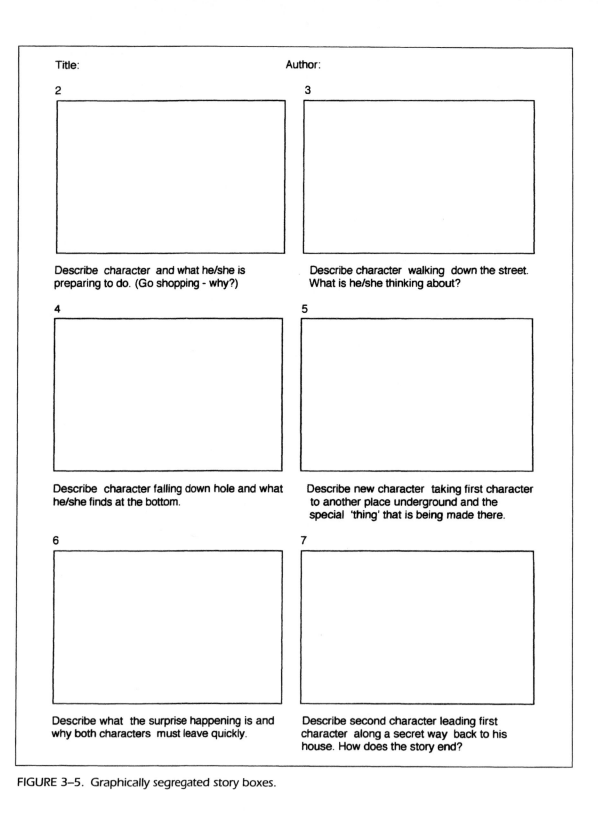

Title: _____   Author: _____

2

Describe character and what he/she is preparing to do. (Go shopping - why?)

3

Describe character walking down the street. What is he/she thinking about?

4

Describe character falling down hole and what he/she finds at the bottom.

5

Describe new character taking first character to another place underground and the special 'thing' that is being made there.

6

Describe what the surprise happening is and why both characters must leave quickly.

7

Describe second character leading first character along a secret way back to his house. How does the story end?

FIGURE 3–5. Graphically segregated story boxes.

Title: _____   Author: _____

2

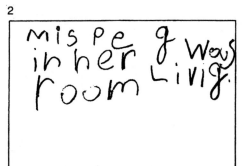

mis pe g was
in her living.
room

Describe character and what he/she is
preparing to do. (Go shopping - why?)

3

she went
shopping
for sum
Bread

Describe character walking down the street.
What is he/she thinking about?

4

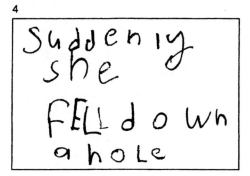

Suddenly
she
FELL down
a hole

Describe character falling down hole and what
he/she finds at the bottom.

5

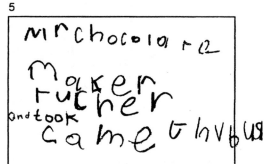

mr chocolare
Maker
and took ruther
came t hv hus

Describe new character taking first character
to another place underground and the
special 'thing' that is being made there.

6

the chocola
re
machihg
BLOON UP

Describe what the surprise happening is and
why both characters must leave quickly.

7

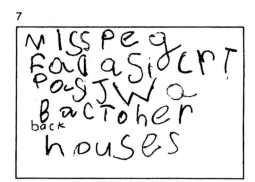

MISS peg
fad a siurt
pous JW a
back Bac Toher
houses

Describe second character leading first
character along a secret way back to his
house. How does the story end?

FIGURE 3–6. James's completed story boxes.

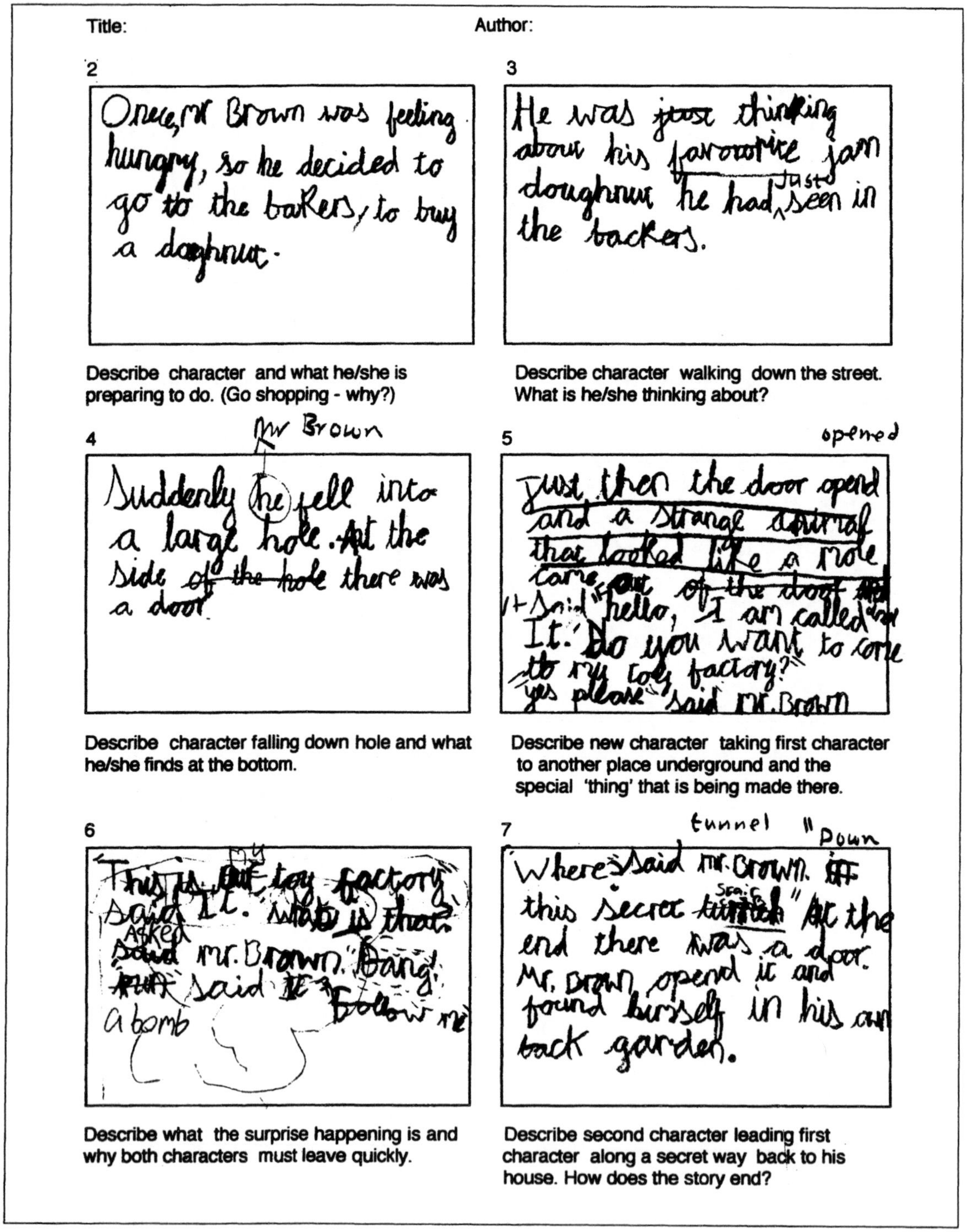

Title: _____   Author: _____

2

> Once, Mr Brown was feeling hungry, so he decided to go to the bakers, to buy a doughnut.

Describe character and what he/she is preparing to do. (Go shopping - why?)

3

> He was just thinking about his favourite jam doughnut he had just seen in the bakers.

Describe character walking down the street. What is he/she thinking about?

4   Mr Brown

> Suddenly he fell into a large hole. At the side of the hole there was a door.

Describe character falling down hole and what he/she finds at the bottom.

5   opened

> Just then the door opened and a strange animal that looked like a mole came out of the door and said "hello, I am called It. Do you want to come to my toy factory?" "yes please" said Mr. Brown

Describe new character taking first character to another place underground and the special 'thing' that is being made there.

6

> This is my toy factory said It. what is that asked said Mr. Brown. "Bang" said It. follow me a bomb

Describe what the surprise happening is and why both characters must leave quickly.

7   tunnel   "Down

> "Where" said Mr. Brown. "this secret tunnel space" At the end there was a door. Mr. Brown opened it and found himself in his own back garden.

Describe second character leading first character along a secret way back to his house. How does the story end?

FIGURE 3–7. Aarash's completed story boxes.

Title: _____   Author   biscuits

2

whether

Mrs Peters was out of Coffee
so she decided to go to
Gateway to get some
more.

Describe character and what he/she is
preparing to do. (Go shopping - why?)

3

As She was walking down
the street she was
wondering weather She Should
get some biscits while
She was out.

Describe character walking down the street.
What is he/she thinking about?

4

Mrs Peters suddenly fell
down a hole. At the bottom
there was a shining door
with a key on the floor.

Describe character falling down hole and what
he/she finds at the bottom.

5

appeared

A man apeared behind
Mrs Peters, and Picked up
the key and opened the door.
Then he said to Mrs Peters
"Come this way" and he said
"his name is Michael".

Describe new character taking first character
to another place underground and the
special 'thing' that is being made there.

6

where

Michael took Mrs Peters through
the door and into a room
were machines were making
burgers and Chips. The burgers
and chips came to life, so
Michael and Mrs Peters went through
another door.   ran

Describe what the surprise happening is and
why both characters must leave quickly.

7

Michael took Mrs Peters up
Some steps back into her
Kitchen through a trap door.
Michael said "Goodbye". and
Mrs Peters went to buy
Some Coffee but she made sure
she didnt fall down the hole again.

Describe second character leading first
character along a secret way back to his
house. How does the story end?

FIGURE 3–8. Katherine's completed story boxes.

FIGURE 3–9. Book layout template.

spatial arrangement of the three double-page spreads and the front and back covers. The prevailing pattern is to alternate illustration/text with text/illustration (pages 4 and 5 show the text and illustration incorporated into the framed area). For variety, this arrangement is inverted for pages 6 and 7.

Making the book from the drafts and sketches is not simply a matter of transferring material, although that in itself would be very satisfying. The larger spaces for illustrations require a different approach to drawing, and the cramped draft narrative is released on the book pages.

James's finished book (Figure 3–10) shows what a liberating effect the larger spatial area has had on him. For example, his confused bottom-of-the-hole-sketch (page 4) becomes a confidently drawn book-page illustration. His sketch for the sequence in the chocolate factory has the two characters colliding, but in the finished illustration they relate to each other at a carefully considered interval. (This is an example of "spatial dynamics," which is discussed in Chapter 6; if the figures are too close there is confusion, if they are too far apart they appear to have no relationship. Balanced on each side of the central pivotal point, they appear to be talking to each other.) In his final book James has also raised the figures into a more horizontally central position so that we see whole figures against a middle ground. These more developed drawings would not have been produced without the preliminary sketches.

The same progress can be seen in Aarash's book (see Figure 3–11). For example, Mr. Brown's top hat in the first box of the sketch has disappeared. In the book it logically appears for the first time on Mr. Brown's head in the exterior scene on the next page. The small sketch of the street scene has prepared the way for the rich composition of the finished picture. It is doubtful whether Aarash would have filled the space with so many interesting pieces of information without his sketch. The figure on page 4 is drawn in a falling position. (Aarash used a movable figure made with paper fasteners—see page 97—as a model.) Notice also the imaginative addition of underground pipes in the final version. Page 6 in the book uses size in a symbolic way: in the sketch, the large drawing of Mr. Brown makes the explosion look small; however, in the book he is drawn as a small figure in the top right corner, thus giving greater emphasis ("weight") to the explosion.

In most of the illustrations for her book (see Figure 3–12), Katherine divides the pictorial area into spatial zones. The bottom half is drawn as foreground (near to the viewer) and the top half as middle ground (further from the viewer). Consequently, she is able to depict specific areas of interest. When the figures need to be shown running (see the next-to-the-

FIGURE 3-10. James's finished book.

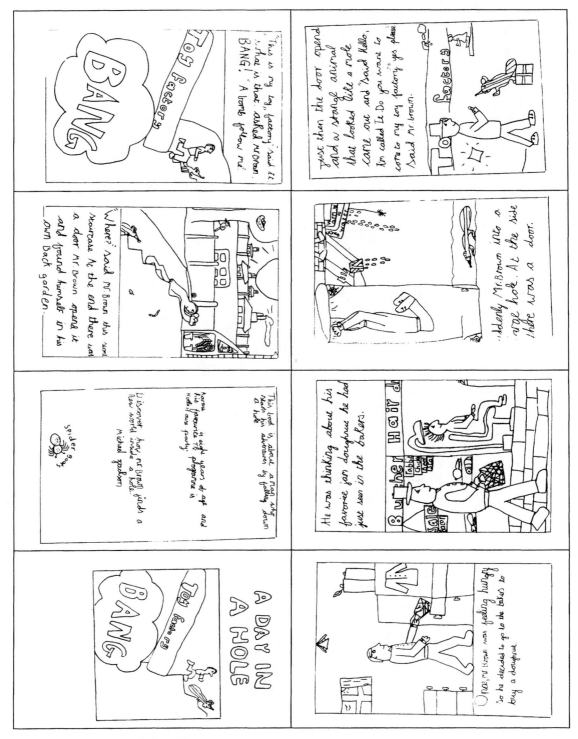

FIGURE 3–11. Aarash's finished book.

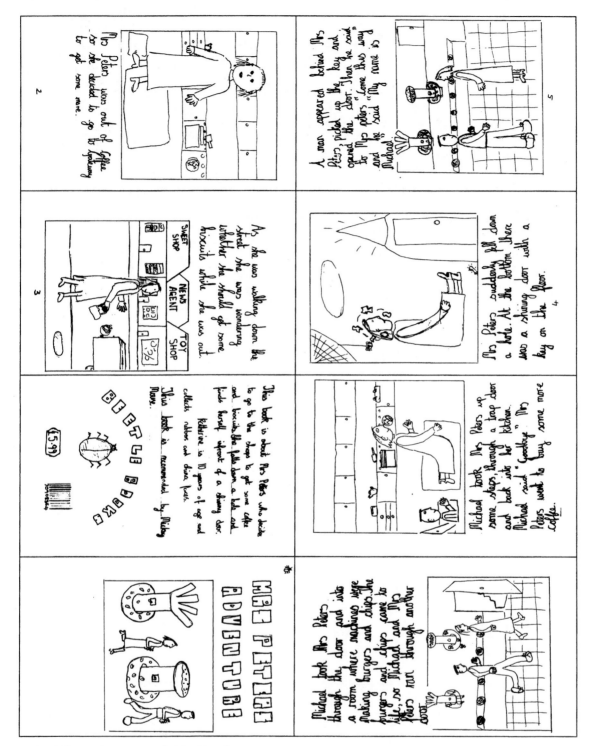

FIGURE 3–12. Katherine's finished book.

last illustration), Katherine indicates movement by increasing the angle of the woman's legs and, with more sophistication, bending the man's legs at the knees. (Like Aarash, Katherine used paper-fastened figures to help her here.) This is in total contrast to the stilled composition of her final illustration.

Experiencing Success

The systematic planning of this picture storybook accelerated writing and picture making for these students. The careful unfolding and refining of the written and visualized narrative, checked and reworked at each stage as necessary, ultimately led to the finished form as one fused, intelligent, and resourceful expression. But let me allow the students to speak for themselves:

I liked thinking up Mrs. Peg and making up a story all about her. . . . My favorite drawing is her coming up the secret passageway into her house. . . . I would like to make a book all about an airplane journey. And I'd like to make one at home too. —JAMES

The more you draw in a picture the more things come to you to put in it. . . . I think it's hard to draw a person falling down a hole because you don't know what it really looks like, but the paper figures helped a lot. . . . I would like to write about what happened to Mr. Brown after he got home again. . . . I really enjoyed making this book and I would like to make many more. It's much more fun than just writing in a ready-made book. —AARASH

I think I could have made the clothes that the people in my story are wearing more interesting. . . . I could have put more things in the kitchen instead of all those empty cupboards. . . . I'm quite happy with the story, but if I did it again I would like it to be a bigger book so that more things could go on in the room with the machines. . . . I would like to call my next book "Life Underground". . . . What is special about these books is that they are like real books—you can show them to people. I think it is one of the best things I have made since I've been at school. —KATHERINE

4

Planning the Writing and Illustrating Process

THE BOOK-ART APPROACH TO REFINING AND VISUALIZING TEXTS

[Children] test out their versions of the world through fantasy and confirm how the world actually is by imagining how it might be different. In the language classroom this capacity for fantasy and imagination has a very constructive part to play.   —SUSAN HALLIWELL

Children can't begin making books too early, and to make one they must know what a book is and how it works. To explore the concept of book, children need a systematic plan of action that will help them solve the problems they will encounter. Here is a suggested ten-point plan of action under three main headings:

PREPARATION

1. Making the book form.
2. Outlining the narrative and specifying the audience.
3. Structuring the story.
4. Drafting the narrative sequences.
5. Editing.

PRODUCTION

6. Laying out a page design.
7. Transferring text.

8. Making illustrations.

9. Designing the cover.

PRESENTATION

10. Publishing, sharing, and developing along a continuum.

Step 1: Making the Book Form

Children need a container for their ideas. Therefore, they should first make or be given a book form. The concertina or origami book (see the appendix) is a good place to start. This concrete object has a quite amazing effect on children's cognition, as these teachers discovered:

> *I thought that one basic book for each child would be enough, but by playtime they were full and they were demanding more.*
>
> *Sebastian, who has severe learning difficulties, asked for another a book to write in. I was astonished.*
>
> *As soon as their little origami books were finished they took them around the nursery to show everybody. They were very proud of them.*

Children are also influenced by the quality of paper they make their books from. Cheap, thin paper is fine for experimental work and drafts, but not for finished products. If we want quality writing, we must provide quality materials, especially for those books that are weeks in the making.

Step 2: Outlining the Narrative and Specifying the Audience

The genesis of storywriting

Our notion of story derives from our experience. Ask a child of five to "make a story" and you will get *The Three Bears* or something similar: because her skills of invention are limited, she retells a known story or recounts a personal experience. Older children take familiar story characters, situations, and settings and reassemble them. Snow White, for example, goes shopping, has a party for her friends, or meets a ghost.

With growing confidence and encouragement in conjuring up new plots based on known ones, children continue a familiar story by using the same characters (possibly creating new ones as well) and constructing "the next episode." Or they may take a character or situation from the historical period they are studying and rework it as a story. This kind of writing demands historical accuracy in the telling.

We loosely think of fictional narratives as "adventures," but as the examples of children's work in this book show, they can be conceived in many ways and in myriad styles, from humorous cartoons to semifictionalized autobiography to stories with a strong moral content.

"New" stories are really difficult for children to write. The real-life people and situations adult writers encounter inevitably color what they write. But children, unable to stand outside themselves and analyze their relationships with others in the way adults do, tend to construct plots from snippets gleaned from children's books and the electronic media. Therefore, unless you watch a lot of children's television shows and videos or play a lot of computer games, it is almost impossible to know whether children have invented their story characters themselves or whether they have come from these electronic sources. However, with time and good teaching, pupils learn to shape a plot of their own.

Story protagonists and settings

I start many of my storybook projects with these questions: Who's our story going to be about? Where does it take place? Well-rounded, convincing characters and clearly identified settings are essential to plot development, but with young children these characterizations are often symbolic—"a man" rather than a specific man, "a house" rather than a house with sharply defined attributes.

The characters in many children's stories are undeveloped and used iconically as vehicles for the story, "someone for things to happen to." Visualizing a realistic imaginary person requires practice. From "a man" to "a magician" to "a magician called Mr. Spells" can take anything from a few minutes to several weeks of storymaking. And the age of the student has little to do with it. Eleven-year-olds with stunted creative experiences can be poorer at putting story characters together than children half their age who have a well-developed imagination.

The book-art approach to storymaking provides its own ways to help children conceive characters. For example, drawing the character before writing about him or her will influence how that character is later described in words.

Storytelling

Storywriting and storytelling are organically intertwined. Taking part in story improvisations, suggesting story plots to and discussing them with their peers, is essential to children's social and oral development. This should be seen in the wider context of our storytelling heritage, of teacher and student retelling favorite folktales or contemporary stories, so that children share in the oral tradition of their own and other cultures and through discussion learn what makes a good story.

Children's literature

Books children make are not unlike the books they read, both in terms of design and content. The more kinds of fiction and nonfiction experienced through shared reading, the greater children's knowledge of what a book is and, with teacher guidance, how books work.

The landscape or portrait orientation of the book form (see the appendix) controls where blocks of text and illustrations are placed on the page. Professional illustrators use all kinds of compositional techniques to make a particular visual fit a space. (For example, if a book with a portrait orientation has a half page of text followed by a half-page illustration, the illustration will be presented landscape.) Children must learn to match a scene to a shape, just as they may have to condense a written narrative episode to fit a prescribed area.

As Roger Beard (1984) points out, children become aware of "story grammars" by having stories read to them; these stories acquaint them with common structural elements like formal beginnings and endings and events that share the same time or space sequence. Getting beneath the surface of a book to what is implied but not said, discussing the "problem" facing a character and predicting possible outcomes, and generally becoming aware of the art of prose writing is the surest foundation to the students' own writing. In the context of modeling writing forms, an awareness of different styles of narrative writing (writing in the first or third person, for example) familiarizes children with the choices they can make.

Collaborative authorship

The book form provides excellent opportunities for students to work together on a shared project. Strategies vary from child A writing and child B illustrating the whole book, to child A writing and illustrating the first spread, child B writing and illustrating the second spread, and so on. If the book extends to several pages, the task assignments can be repetitive or students can negotiate them page by page.

A whole table of, say, six children can also contribute to the same book, becoming in effect a production team. As only one child can work in the book at any one time, some elements will necessarily be created on separate sheets of paper and pasted in when finished. The conceiving, drafting, and editing stages and the overall delegation of tasks provide a range of interactive challenges for those involved.

Form and content

While most children are enthusiastic about writing stories, they do not necessarily find the process an easy one. It is common for children to devise stories that have form but no content or content but no form.

An example of the former is what has come to be known as the *bed-to-*

bed story: "John got up, got dressed, went outside and played football, then he went swimming, then he came home and went to bed." There is an A B A shape to this plot—leaving home, doing something, then returning home—but the events are prosaic and there is no development. In this kind of story "the day" is the limit of the child's concept of time and thus dictates the parameters of the plot.

Conversely, it is not unusual for children to link unusual events in quick succession but for the story line to be formless: "One day John decided to rob a bank. When he got to the bank it was full of aliens who returned to Mars in their spaceship. When they got there they found that some aliens were having a party on Venus. . . ."

Integrating strong form and imaginative content is the art of storywriting.

Climbing over clichés

A major preoccupation with teaching is releasing children from the clichés that ensnare their writing. In the narrative genre (and with children of almost any age) brainstorming characters and plots is excellent preparation. Apart from providing valuable social and interpersonal experience, it suggests story outlines to those students who struggle with them and new and original twists to texts already formulated.

From verbalizing to writing

Children soon discover that it is one thing to "make up a story" and another to write it down. Writing imposes its own logic and sensibility. Uri Shulevitz, in *Writing with Pictures* (1985), his detailed and fascinating analysis of his own work, describes how a good storybook can entertain and have meaningful human interest, social significance, and aesthetic appeal. Creating excitement, introducing credible characters, coming up with the unexpected, and finding satisfactory conclusions in simple yet imaginative prose are the objectives of all authorship regardless of the age of the author.

Audience awareness

Just as good actors usually direct their performance to one person in the audience, so professional authors aim their book at a particular kind of child. Children who can conceive a specific audience for their work have the pleasure of writing for an identified group or individual. Although they are not aware of it, they are developing a highly sophisticated attitude to writing.

Step 3: Structuring the Story

The fixed-page book

Stories have shape. Simplistically they are defined as having a beginning (premise), a middle (development), and an end (resolution). A book with a set number of pages, like the six-page origami book, prescribes a story to fit it. Jessica's story *Christmas Eve* (see Figure 4–1) shows how processing each item of her story on a designated page has expedited clear and precise thinking. (Similarly, in Chapter 2, Tim spring-cleans his untidy story by consciously planning his plot to fit a fixed-page book.)

As children become more sophisticated in conceiving plots "in a book way" the predetermined page arrangements condition how plots evolve. For example, Omamah's book in Figure 4–2 has an A AB AB A format—an initial page of writing, followed by two spreads of left-side text, right-side illustration, followed by a final page of writing. The first illustration of Marcia inside a milkshake bottle has to coordinate with the description

FIGURE 4–1. Nine-year-old Jessica's story.

on the facing page of how she got there; the beginning of the story written on the previous page therefore has to lead into this description. So Omamah begins by setting the scene, describing Marcia delivering milkshakes "which all the children love," before getting into the main thrust of the plot on the next page. The next text-illustration spread is the climax of the story, in which Marcia has a wonderful time in Milkshake Land—we see her riding in a milkshake car. The overleaf, the final page of text, winds up her adventure (on the top half of page) and returns her safely to

FIGURE 4–2. Eight-year-old Omamah's book.

Marcia, the milk lady enjoys delivering milk shakes which all the children love. She makes many flavours, like rasberry, strawberry, banana and chocolate. She delivers them every morning to children everywhere.
One bright morning

as Marcia was delivering a strawberry milkshake she tripped over and fell into the bottle. She found herself in strawberry milkshakeland. She saw some milkshake cars and milkshake shops, and in the shops there were milkshakes!...

She saw strawberry people, cats and dogs. There were strawberry houses too.. She had a lovely time in milkshake land. She drank lots of brightly coloured milk= shake in the milkshake shop, and rode in the cars

made from milkshake. She met some strawberry people, and talked to them, but they spoke in strawberry language, and Marcia didn't understand it. Marcia had a lovely time, but then she realized that she had to go back and be normal again. So she returned to delivering milkshakes every morning.

delivering milkshakes (the final sentence). Note how this last page fits Omamah's plan like a glove—only a centimeter or so to spare!

The extended book

One of the charms of the concertina book form is that it can be extended to any length by adding extra sections. Skill in writing both the fixed-paged and the unrestricted-page book is valuable; freedom and restriction are each necessary to creativity. As the teacher you decide which kind to use based on the project at hand, the students involved, and the learning objectives.

Story and book together

Clearly, it will help children if their story ideas and the book form selected to hold them are combined in the formative stages. One way to do this is to hold the book form in your hands and turn the pages as your students improvise and discuss successive story episodes. This helps the children identify which parts of their story will occupy the designated pages.

Text and illustration

It is much easier to fit artwork to the text than vice versa; so it is useful at this stage if children have a rough idea of where the words of the story are to go. The simplest structure is to alternate whole pages of writing with whole pages of illustration (the books used as examples in Chapter 2 use this format).

A half page of writing combined with a half-page illustration (six successive sequences in the basic book form) is a more demanding format because the child has to plan more sequences, must use fewer words in each section, and has to create more illustrations. (This format was illustrated in Chapter 3.)

Step 4: Drafting Narrative Sequences

Lucy Calkins (1986) stresses the importance of the drafting process: writing is not simply a matter of putting down one's thoughts and ideas for immediate publication. There are many personal and social considerations, and each teacher takes a very individual approach to this nurturing period. However, working in a book-oriented way influences how writing strategies are implemented.

Emergent writers usually work directly in their books. Some children will think "in a page way" instinctively, while others will need book-making experiences before they learn to think in episodes. *In situ* drafting is a kind of halfway house between as-is publication and edited drafts.

Here, pupils, write directly on the book pages using soft pencils, then make changes to the text by erasing words or phrases and correcting or replacing them. Of course, interacting with other students, exploring collaborative modes of authorship, and sharing the emerging book with partners and groups are essential to the holistic process.

As pupils grow in skills and confidence, they are ready to prepare writing in one form for presentation in another. Teachers often argue that children don't want to write a story twice, first as a draft and then in final "published" form. But Donald Graves (1983) insists that students setting out to write something in published form are able to give meaning to the preparatory stages as well. The attraction of the book form—which is designed to be shared with others and cherished as an aesthetic object—is that it gives a reason for drafting, rewriting, and presenting.

Children for whom an extended piece of drafting would be too demanding or who become impatient with getting on with the book can draft, edit, and transfer each episode to the book one at a time. The satisfaction of finishing a page can be an incentive to completing the rest of the book.

Storyboards

Chapter 3 shows how very prescriptive storyboards can be used to provide a book structure, but a simple row of boxes can also be an effective aid in planning sequences. Keeley's story in Figure 4–3 was created on a sheet of six empty boxes. It recounts the interaction of a boy and a kite, who are introduced separately and then go on a journey. The climax of the narrative is reached in box 5, when the boy lets go of the kite, but resolved in the next (and final) sequence, when the boy gets the kite back.

Using a book planner (see Figure 4–4) is another way to help children organize basic plot episodes and link them to illustrations. A chalkboard diagram of the book pages (see Figure 4–5) can reinforce the book plan and be used in conjunction with the personal storyboard.

Storyboards can be designed in many ways using regular or irregular shapes and any number of boxes. Icons like circles and "explosions" can be used to suggest plot developments. An especially useful feature of any storyboard variation is that the children see all the story episodes as one diagrammatic whole.

Book "dummies"

The physical presence of the book form often inspires and stimulates children to write. *In situ* drafting enables a student to prepare a text in the finished book, but for more experienced authors there is no reason the draft should not be done in the same form as the final book but, say, on much cheaper paper. This is, after all, the way professional author/illustrators plan a book—laying the "dummy" out in the same page configurations as the finished product. The dummy also functions as a quality assessment; students can appraise their book in total before the final realization.

Templates

A draft should be as close to the finished format as possible. Drafting and editing within a rectangular template drawn in the center of a sheet of paper allows room in the margins to sketch possible illustrations and note suggestions and corrections. Ten-year-old Ellicia used this technique in the drafts shown in Figure 4–6. The first two show the evolving narrative as battleground. However, as Ellicia gets closer to a plot she's happy with (her third draft), fewer doodles appear in the margins.

Brackets

Some students prefer to write their draft in a conventional exercise book and then bracket off the sections they will transfer to book pages. Ten-

FIGURE 4–3. Five-year-old Keeley's sequence of boxes.

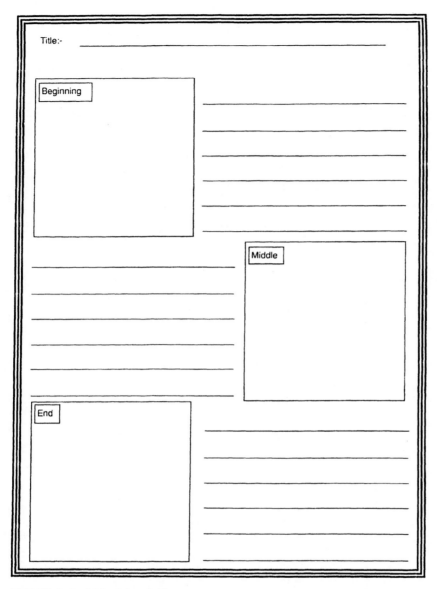

FIGURE 4–4. A blank book planner.

year-old Vicki uses this technique in the example in Figure 4–7. The technique is particularly useful when creating a concertina book, which can extend into an infinite number of pages.

Picture references

In this technique, the author uses small thumbnail sketches as visual full stops at the end of episodes. These miniatures express only a figurative outline—the essence of the episode—that helps the author concentrate and

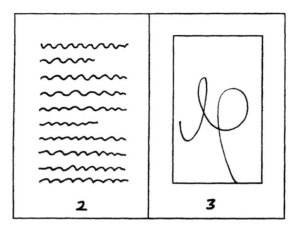

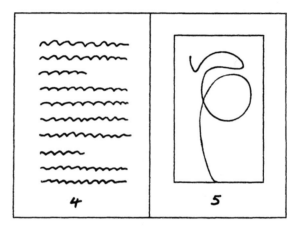

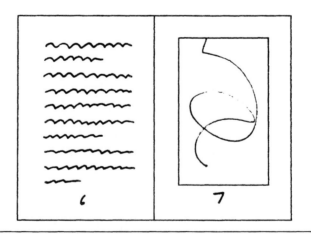

FIGURE 4–5. Chalkboard storyboard diagram.

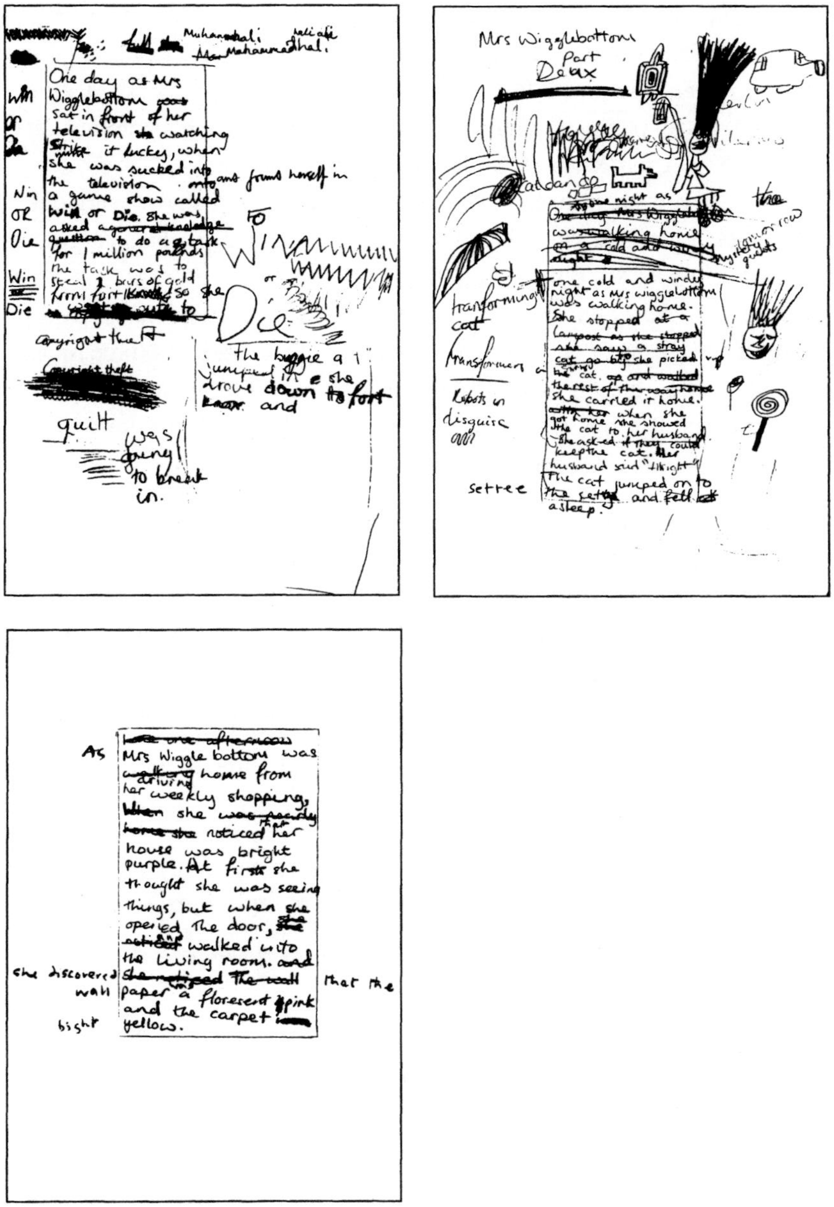

FIGURE 4–6. Ellicia's drafts using a page template.

ultimately helps him or her plan the book page by page. Six-year-old Andreas uses this technique in the draft shown in Figure 4–8.

Computer graphics and word processing

Books written using computer word processing and graphics programs can be drafted, edited, and published in the same venue. (Alternatively, the edited printout can be cut and pasted into a book form.)

However, while computer graphics programs offer the illustrator quite astonishing visual effects, very few children's picture-book illustrators use them. The electronic image fails in one often essential aspect—the tactile and emotional experience of physically applying paint and graphite, of using brush, pen, and scissors. Some things don't change.

With help from their teacher, Latricia and David, both seven years old, produced the illustration in Figure 4–9 using a computer graphics program and then word-processed their drafted text.

The text of the collaboratively produced narrative *The Trip to Egypt* (see Figure 4–10) was composed on a computer. Printing it out three times provided each of the three nine-year-old authors with the same text but gave them each the opportunity to draw her or his own illustrations. (The initial page spreads from two books are shown.)

The comic-book approach

Children are attracted by the speech bubbles in advertising and comics and love to use it in their own books. In the example in Figure 4–11, John tells his story entirely through the speech bubbles emerging from his characters' mouths. The football instructor's pronouncements and the snail's asides are funny and successfully integrated. Both characters have their own territory

FIGURE 4–7. Brackets indicate which text will be transferred to which book page.

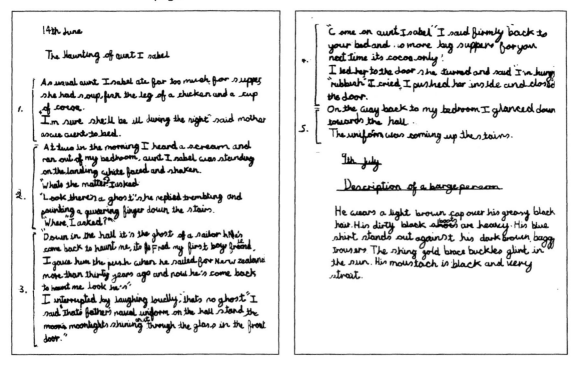

The prehistoric World.
One day I was walking when
I fell down a hole. I found
myself in a prehistoric
world. I was looking around
when I saw a t-rex.
It looked like it was chasing
Somthing. Then I saw him chasing
a smaller dinosaur. The smaller
dinosaur was runing to me it came
closer. Now t-rex was going to stamp
on me. Quickly I moved away.
Then it was out of sight

FIGURE 4–8. Thumbnail illustration references.

(footballer, top half of panel; snail, bottom half), so there is enough space for the figures and the speech bubbles to be clearly presented.

It can be argued that speech is expressed more directly through the speech bubble than through the punctuation symbols of conventional written dialogue. Sheila Lane (1984) says that as well as helping children think socially, the "thinking clouds" and speech bubbles of cartoons underline the interaction between thinking and speaking and reinforce the relationship between spoken and written language. The cartoonist Gary Larson (1995) suggests that it is risky to accompany cartoons with long captions because they take you too far away from the static image. Much the same goes for storyboard narratives and, indeed, any genre that closely integrates words and pictures; the eye needs to bounce back and forth between word forms and picture images.

FIGURE 4–9. Page layout using the computer.

Poetry

Any discussion of children making storybooks must include the most refined form of writing, poetry. Poetry and illustration have a long history of cohabiting in book form. First, they are both visually aesthetic "objects," and second, the thin word block leaves ample space for artwork.

Because poems (other than epics) tend to be short, often extending no more than a page, they sit within the page rectangle as a carefully designed arrangement of words. Children writing poems are freed from the page-by-page sequencing challenge of narrative, but face instead the perhaps greater challenge of using words with economical precision.

In the example in Figure 4–12, Beth has used several different design patterns to integrate a few carefully chosen words with line illustrations.

Step 5: Editing

Verbal-exchange editing

Very young children edit via verbal exchanges. This is a time of celebrating story ideas aloud, of self-verification. "This is what my book is going to be about" is stated proudly and indefatigably around the table. Conversation helps clarify thought and can bring about a change of emphasis. Discussion and reflection allow children to refine their plot statements before they are recorded in the book via invented or assisted writing, as dictated to the teacher, or perhaps solely with images.

Personal editing

If children are drafting texts, then it logically follows that they are ready to edit them as well. Writers are so busy writing that incorrect grammar and spelling easily creep in. Reading through the whole story, or an episode, children switch from *invention* to *assessment*. They need to question the "success" of their plot as a gripping yarn and check the mechanics (spelling, for example, and, if appropriate, things like quotation marks—always a minefield for children). Very often children know that a sentence is "wrong" without knowing why. Periodic workshops during this drafting/editing phase in basic secretarial skills, composition (avoiding

FIGURE 4–10. Computer-generated text of *The Trip to Egypt*.

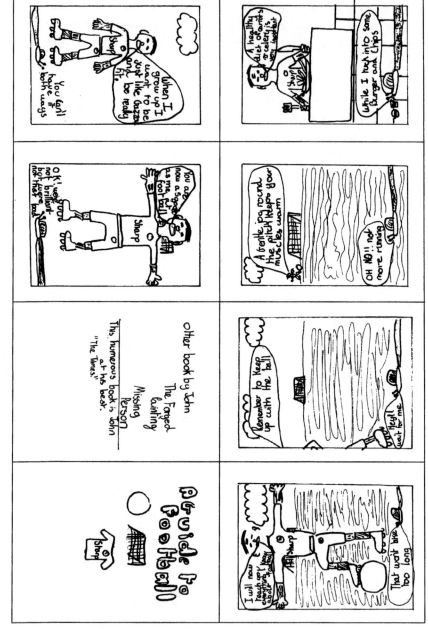

FIGURE 4–11. Nine-year-old John's *A Guide to Football.*

repetition, for example), and presentation styles can help students work through their own quality assessment.

Shared editing

An important development in the craft of writing occurs when pupils read completed story sections to their partner and invite suggestions for

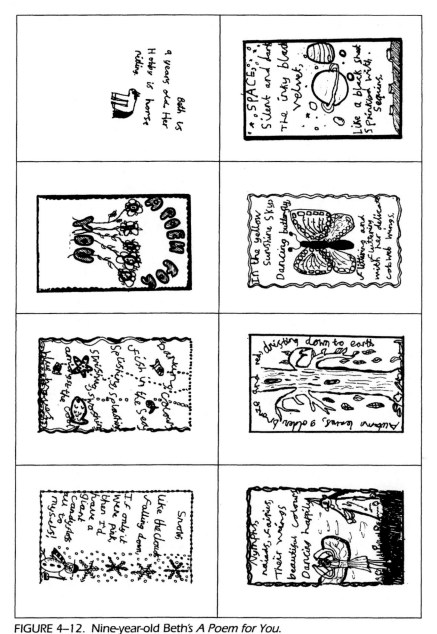

FIGURE 4–12. Nine-year-old Beth's A Poem for You.

improvements. More experienced editing partners read each other's work and make comments. Developing the critical skills of editing is as valuable as developing the ability to write creatively and fluently. Pairing a less able student with a more able one ensures that while the less able is gaining constructive advice, the more able is developing the critical acumen required for the task.

Of course every child rarely gains equally from every editing exercise.

Groupings need to be varied so that every pupil gets a fair share of the particular assistance or experience she or he needs.

Some of the questions editors should ask about stories they are reading are:

- Is the main character interesting?
- Is each page of writing clear?
- Does the beginning of the story excite me enough to turn the page?
- Is the middle part of the story lively enough?
- Is the story ending satisfying and appealing?
- Is the whole story entertaining and varied?

There are many approaches to drafting, editing, and revising, to the teacher's role as "editor in chief," and to controversial issues such as how moral questions and the sexism, racism, and ageism that creep into children's narratives should be addressed.

There are many ways of teaching handwriting, and each school will have its own approach to doing so. Some teachers accept (indeed encourage) poor handwriting at this stage because, they argue, children need to feel their writing is only at the sketch stage—they need the freedom to write spontaneously and not worry about legibility. Teachers who place high priority on developing the creative imagination of pupils stand back from incorrect grammar, spelling, and punctuation at the drafting stage because a good story is all that matters and corrections can be made in the editing.

(Obviously, shy or noncommunicative children need special help at this stage, as do those with special needs and learning difficulties. Figure 4–13 is a spread from a book by Pamela, a special-needs student. Pamela discussed each part of her story with her teacher—who described the process as "a verbal refining of the narrative"—before writing it in book form. This book was a landmark in Pamela's development.)

Whereas drafting is a more private concern, editing tends to be more public. Students who produce confidently penned yet stereotypical stories need as much help as those with no ideas at all. Both are waiting for that wonderful moment when the heart of a story begins to beat. The final stage of editing, when the teacher is satisfied that for this student the narrative structure is successful and reasonably free of mechanical error, should be a time of real satisfaction for both child author and teacher.

Step 6: Laying Out a Page Design

At this point it's time to return to the book form (although it should never have been far from the scene of operations). Children now bring their

FIGURE 4–13. A spread from Pamela's story.

books from the back to the front of the table and place their final edited draft behind it. The page design strategy discussed or planned during the preparatory stages must now be applied to the finished book: page templates are drawn, and text and illustration areas designated.

The imagination generates mental pictures that accompany verbally conceived stories. But it is infinitely harder to define an imagined object as a drawing than to write the word for it. Processing text demands a different set of skills from those needed to process illustrations. Some children will have a strong urge to draw a scene from their story before writing it. Those more reticent about drawing, particularly older students, might feel the opposite pull and need special encouragement regarding their illustrations. I find that most children want to write and draw the page spreads chronologically. Book-art projects need the flexibility to encompass all working patterns.

Step 7: Transferring Text

If the text has been drafted with the final book in mind, the blocks of words should fit the pages reasonably well. Teachers have different views about how corrections should be dealt with at this stage. Some teachers, especially of younger children, require them to write in pencil. Others let their students use ink as a special reward. (You could ask students to write in pencil first and make any final corrections before going over everything in ink, but this is a chore; it's better to let them write directly in ink and use correction fluid to correct any mistakes.)

In any case, if each book page of writing is seen as an aesthetic object to be enjoyed as much for its appearance as for what it says, children should experience pride and pleasure in producing it.

Step 8: Making Illustrations

The illustrator exists by virtue of having stories to illustrate. David Bland (1958) makes the point that the illustrator depends far more on the author than vice versa. I recently attended a seminar in which a professional writer/illustrator said she created illustrations based on a story outline and these illustrations then triggered ideas that caused the story to be changed; nevertheless, it was the written story that was pivotal.

Children are in this same situation. They have to decide what parts of their narratives suggest the best images. Action of one kind or another translates well visually, so it is important for children to learn to draw people in motion (see Chapter 5). But stillness can be just as effective. For example Raisa's illustration of the interior of a room (page 72) holds the eye with its color and pattern, and Edward's drawing of an antique shop exterior (page 108) entices us because of the complexity of his design.

What is essential is variety. One of the problems facing the young illustrator is how to redraw the same character over and over again without resorting to repetition.

In his book *The Explorer* (see Figure 4–14), seven-year-old Jamie draws the eponymous protagonist differently each time he is portrayed. The first full-page illustration shows him walking side-view out of the picture, which projects us forward into the next page. This page is half text and half illustration, so Jamie had to include both the jaguar and the explorer in a smaller space. His solution was to place the explorer's head on the base of the frame, thus leaving ample horizontal space for the jaguar. In the next panel Jamie draws a back view of the explorer watching TV. On the overleaf he is riding on the back of the jaguar, and the final illustration is of both characters sitting obliquely on the ground having a picnic.

Jamie has also neatly woven the text around the pictures—no two pages have the same design. He uses the illustration areas to the fullest: the top of the first full-page illustration shows the jaguar crouching on a branch; later, the image of the explorer riding the jaguar is balanced by the tree to his left and the bird perched on a branch to his right. The diagonals of the tablecloth in the last picture contrast with the predominant verticals and horizontals of the earlier illustrations.

Good stories need involvement and tension, so by the second or third illustration the main character is usually confronted by another person,

FIGURE 4–14. Jamie's story, *The Explorer*.

object, task, or situation. The illustrations are intertwined with the text and develop frame by frame. To vitalize these scenes and keep the eye active, the illustrator varies the composition. This can be done spatially, by moving the figures forward (nearer to us) or back (further away from us) or raising or lowering the horizon line (see Chapter 7) so that the viewer looks down or up on a scene, and environmentally, by varying the locations (street scene, path by a stream), weather conditions (rain, fog), seasons (falling leaves, snowscape), or time of day (full daylight, twilight, nighttime).

Six-year-old Raisa's story (see Figure 4–15) is about a cat who, out for a walk, spots a dog's house. The dog who lives there invites the cat in, takes her on a tour of the house, and invites her to stay for tea. When she leaves she promises to return.

Raisa wrote her text directly into the book form but made *in situ* changes during its composition. In addition to a single page of text at the beginning and at the end, there are two full-page spreads of balanced text and illustration. In talking about her story, Raisa made a verbal list of all the things in the house's interior—"cushions, chairs, rugs, TV, toy cats, and a cupboard"—and this helped her write the room description on the

FIGURE 4–15. Raisa's story, *Frisky and the Dog.*

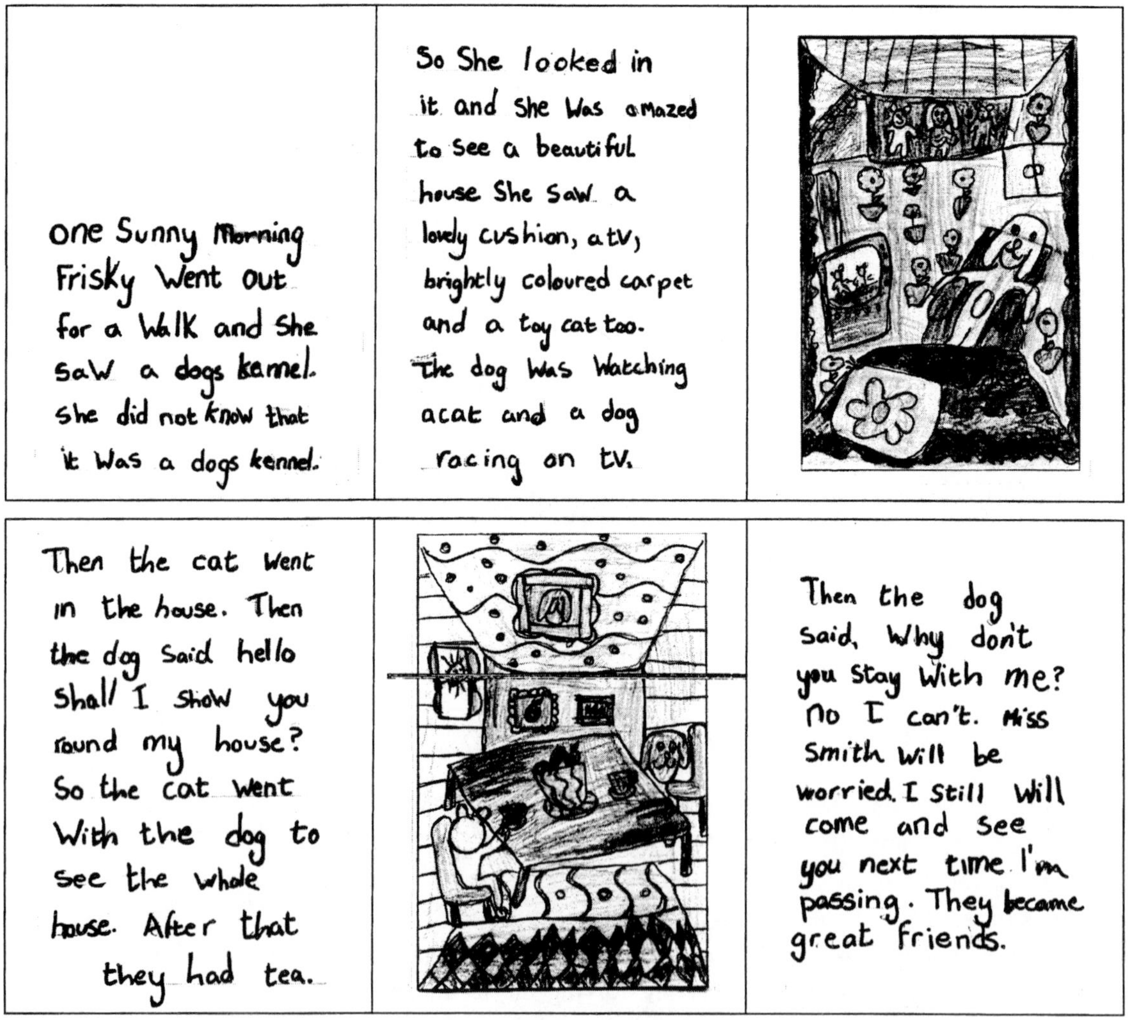

one Sunny morning Frisky Went out for a Walk and She saW a dogs kennel. She did not know that it Was a dogs kennel.

So She looked in it and she Was amazed to See a beautiful house She saW a lovely cushion, a tv, brightly coloured carpet and a toy cat too. The dog Was Watching a cat and a dog racing on tv.

Then the cat Went in the house. Then the dog Said hello Shall I shoW you round my house? So the cat Went With the dog to see the whole house. After that they had tea.

Then the dog said, Why don't you Stay With me? no I can't. Miss Smith will be worried. I still Will come and see you next time I'm passing. They became great friends.

second page and create the matching illustration. In her first attempt she placed the dog on the base line, but after talking with her teacher about spatial relationships she drew the cushion and rug in the bottom part of the picture, the dog in the middle, and the cupboard holding the toy cats at the top, taking her ability as an illustrator to a new level.

The abstract skill of "designing" a picture or plot is hard for children; they find it very difficult to make an outline of a story or sketch a picture. In her second illustration, in which the cat and dog are shown having tea together, Raisa has divided the composition into three parts—foreground, rug; middle ground, table; and background, rear wall of room—without assistance. There is a sense of place in both writing and illustration here: what Victor Watson (1992) describes as "magical space." We feel sucked into the page spread and for a while live in the imaginary world that this young child has created.

It is impossible to think of children's books minus their illustrations and the part these illustrations play in the child's cognition. Judith Graham (1990) elucidates the role of illustration in arresting some aspect of the narrative episode it accompanies, and, via the spatial complexity of the picture plane, revealing a world of visual meaning. Imagery is opened up to spatial investigation; the viewer looks at what's inside a room, sees what a character is wearing.

But more than providing a still from the story, the illustrator is able to tell stories that are actively envisioned but not actually penned in the narrative. Children need to be nurtured to appreciate and use this visual narrative language in stages.

There is a "grammar" of picture making, just as there are "genres" of pictorial composition. A picture done in colored pencil speaks to the imagination differently than a collage does. A simple exterior scene in watercolor can be as striking as a highly detailed interior in pen and ink.

Most book illustrators exploit color to the fullest, but line work has a beauty and meaning all its own. From a practical point of view, working with just a pen, without having to change paints or crayons, frees the hand to make an uninterrupted statement. Line drawing is a high art. Although learning to use color is an essential aspect of the illustrator's art, the skill of drawing is central to the illustrator's craft. While much has been lost in the black-and-white reproductions of color illustrations in this book, their composition is clearly visible. So much in art depends on real or imagined lines. Visualizing a narrative, deciding what part of an episode to portray, who and what to include in the picture, how to draw them, and where to place them, are skills essential to the author. It is as complex to teach children to do this as it is to teach them to write.

FIGURE 4–16. Some student-designed book covers.

Step 9: Designing the Cover

To complete their book, children add the wrapper—a cover. The design challenge here is very different from the one posed by the interior of the book. Few words are used—on the front cover, a riveting title and the author's name are sufficient. These look better as lettering rather than handwriting.

There are many cover-design formats, but the most common is title at the top, an illustration of a salient feature of the book in the middle, and the author's name at the bottom. The back cover can include a few carefully chosen words "about the author," a synopsis of the book, publisher's advertising blurb, publisher's logo, a "price," and a facsimile of a bar code.

Figure 4–16 shows some representative covers created by children of various ages between five and ten.

Step 10: Publishing, Sharing, and Developing Along a Continuum

With the cover completed, the book is now ready to be published—that is, disseminated to its intended audience. Immediately sharing it with one's editing partner is a nice personal touch. This time of showing one's book to others is wonderfully reassuring. Students feel rightly proud of the results of what can be a lengthy process. There is valuable feedback to be gained at this time: children can write a review of a fellow student's book. Ultimately these books can become class readers or even take an honored place in the school library or as part of a "special collection."

Multiple-copy distribution is also viable. These basic books are easily opened up flat and photocopied. The photocopied sheets can then be folded into the same format as the original.

Every teacher longs for learning to become self-motivated and self-directed. As students finish one book, the outline of the next one should be already forming in their imagination. This can be a sequel using the same characters or something completely different, perhaps an idea generated by a recently read story or by an event in their own life.

It is also important once in a while to turn off a well-worn writing path and head toward new horizons, to subject oneself to other writing experiences and new challenges. So a storybook might be followed by a project book on a historical or an ecological theme, or by a pop-up or removable-parts book, or by a class newspaper.

5

Drawing Story Characters*

PUTTING PEOPLE INTO PICTURES

When [children's] visual sensitivity is undeveloped they tend to focus on one thing at a time and draw quite separate objects surrounded by space. Art can help them to perceive the world in a greatly extended way so that they then begin to assimilate a variety of perceptions in relation one to another. —ROB BARNES

Drawing people and animals is so much harder than drawing inanimate objects like buildings. The eye can never isolate a moment of movement, hold it still, and study it. Children use simplifying techniques to convey the impression of the body shape, stationary or in movement.

To young children, things are what they seem like, smell like, move like, or feel like rather than what they objectively "are." So when a young child portrays himself as a pattern of simple lines, circles, and ovals, it is not so much that he sees himself this way but that this configuration meets his needs. He treats color in the same way. The green of a particular tree in his painting represents the "greenness" of trees.

This is invention, not imitation, the discovery of a shape or color that

I am indebted to Maureen Cox's Children's Drawings (1992), which has informed much of the material in this chapter.

represents the relevant features of a form within the limits of the available materials. *Schema* is the name often given to this phenomenon, but it should not be seen as a kind of mold, as it often is, but as an organic thing always growing and changing. (Of course it is impossible to isolate picture characters from their environments, but for study purposes attention is drawn here to drawing people.)

Scribbles

The first scribbles a child makes (see the example in Figure 5–1) grow from an *expressive* need to move—a form of enjoyable motor activity. But mental qualities are reflected in the kinds of strokes used to make these early marks and the speed and rhythm with which they are executed. (Harste, Woodward, and Burk [1984] believe that these attributes are later also evident in the personal style the child develops in both drawing and handwriting.) The marks also imitate the properties of objects or actions, the largeness or fastness of things.

What makes art so difficult is that while one sees a scene in its entirety, the depiction of it has to be executed within linear time. As children draw, they must constantly refer to what has already been drawn. For example, only when a body shape has been described can bodily appendages like arms and legs be added.

The Circle

The circle is the first organized shape to emerge from scribbles (see Figure 5–2). It is topological; that is, rather than being a depiction of a geometric shape, it refers to the boundary of things. It stands for the totality of all shape until shapes become differentiated. When the circle is used to indicate a human figure, there is much speculation as to what is represented— the whole torso? just the head? Psychologists have various interpretations for this "primordial circle," and it seems to be a universal trait in children's imagery.

Adding to the Circle

As a child matures, the crude circle becomes part of more complex patterns. One such elaboration is the lines that radiate from it, becoming, for example, the sun, fingers on a hand, arms and legs on a body, branches on a tree. The circle is the foundation on which children build their reper-

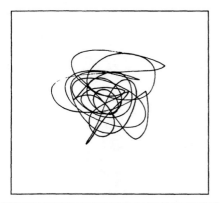

FIGURE 5–1. *An example of a child's first scribbles.*

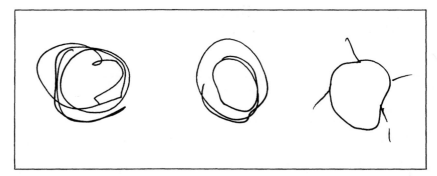

FIGURE 5–2. *The emergence of the circle in a child's drawing.*

toire of images. (The ability to develop these forms depends on children's having the motor control to be able to place marks where they want them to go.)

The Figure

As drawing develops, the isolated symbolic form emerges as a figure placed in a spatial environment for which the edges of the sheet of paper or page are the boundary (see Figure 5–3). Most figures in children's drawings are placed perpendicular to the ground, but children can be persuaded to adapt their drawings to show movement and action.

Vertical and Horizontal Lines

The straight line is visually the simplest of all lines but in fact the hardest to draw; it stands for all elongated shapes and is the most basic expression of movement.

FIGURE 5–3. Four-year-old Umar's figure drawing.

FIGURE 5–4. Vertical and horizontal lines and right angles in six-year-old Michael's drawing.

The child uses vertical and horizontal lines to represent basic concepts like the uprightness of people and trees, and the arms and legs of figures. The right angle—the meeting of a vertical and a horizontal line—is used to represent all angular relationships. (See Figure 5–4.)

At a later phase of development, the oblique line is employed to

FIGURE 5–5. Diagonally drawn legs suggest the movement of a walking figure.

I like Surfing
Said Brilliant
Brian. It's most
out standing Said
Brilliant
Brian,
this is
ace man

now I'm
dripping
wet

Brilliant Brian
came out of
the Sea
dripping wet from
falling in the
water.

FIGURE 5–6. Diagonally drawn legs and arms suggest the body movement of a surfer.

mark the difference between static and dynamic shapes (see Figures 5–5 and 5–6).

It is important not to disturb the cognitive development of children by urging them to attain a higher level of complexity than they are ready for. This emerges progressively. In time children move from drawing single isolated shapes to attaching lines to these shapes to mastering a continuous line flow.

Size

It might seem reasonable to assume that when children draw small things large, it is because of the importance they attach to them. But an equally valid interpretation is that the child is trying to establish a visual relationship between forms.

When young children draw a hand as large as a torso, which they often do, they may be doing it so that it can be more sharply seen. That may also be why Sarah depicts a hedgehog as being as large as her dad (see Figure 5–7).

Side Views and Combined Views

When drawing figures seen from an angle, children often have trouble visualizing what parts are and are not visible. They sometimes get around this problem by drawing a side view (see Figure 5–8). Or they may combine a front view and a side view. (The ancient Egyptians also selected the parts of an object that best suited their pictorial purpose—for example, a front view of a person's chest combined with a side view of the head that included a front view of the eye.) In the illustration in Figure 5–9, Michael has drawn the side view of the cat's torso and legs, a front view of its head,

FIGURE 5–7. Five-year-old Sarah's drawing: "My dad found a hedgehog in our garden."

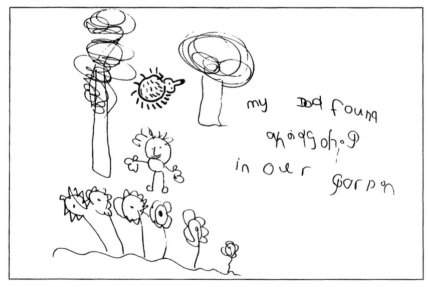

FIGURE 5–8. Five-year-old Judi's drawing of two friends playing a game.

tom the three
leged cat.

by Michael
Greenfield

FIGURE 5–9. Six-year-old Michael's drawing of a three-legged cat.

and a side view of its nose. While not visually "correct," it is nevertheless a sensible way to communicate the appearance of things.

Perspective

A perspective drawing, in which a person standing some distance from another person nearer the foreground appears smaller than that person, is objectively a lie, for both people are in life relatively the same size. Another problem with perspective is that foreground objects often obliterate middle- and background ones.

Presenting forms on one plane, so that front and side views are integrated, or choosing a point of view looking down on a composition, thus flattening the subject matter, increases the amount of visual information conveyed.

Drawing from Life

Skill in observing and analyzing influences children's narrative illustrations. The oil lamp and plant in Helen's illustration in Figure 5–10 were drawn as still lifes, but the figure was drawn from imagination. The accuracy with which Helen was able to record the plant motivated the story it generated.

Just as children widen their knowledge of language by encountering its many spoken and printed forms that surround them, they increase their knowledge of illustration by encountering their seen environment. This includes photographs in magazines, drawings in picture books, the three-dimensional toys they play with, and the images on TV and in computer games. As teachers we long for the time when children will creatively construct wholly invented pictorial compositions derived from a knowledge of the observed world around them.

The Influence of the Comic Strip

The first two pages of nine-year-old Jonathan's story about a pig, Porkpie, who wants to fly, are shown in Figure 5–11. On the first page Porkpie holds us with his glance as if to say, *Hello. I'm the person telling this story and it's all about me!* In the second panel Dennis Duck is looking at us too—his gaze says, *Can you* believe *what this guy is* saying?

It is so easy for children to plagiarize comic-strip mannerisms in their illustrations. Yet students like Jonathan seem to be naturals in the genre and use it convincingly. They have learned that the expression on a character's face can convey a world of meaning.

Using Toys as Models

Paula, a student teacher, was working with a group of ESL students who were playing with a Lego kit. Haniki and Petri, age five, became fascinat-

FIGURE 5–10. "Every day Mary watered her plant."

ed with the Lego horses; they placed figures on them and moved them around the table. They then named the two riders, and with Paula's help, gave them identities and began a story about them: "Once upon a time there was a little village." They alternated drawing the illustrations—Haniki, page 1, Petri, page 2, and so on—and Paula served as scribe (later the text was transferred to a word processor, and the printout attached to the bottom of each page).

The horses were the main thrust of the narrative, and the children used the Lego horses as models for their drawings (when Petri had to draw them galloping away, he positioned them accordingly—see Figure 5–12).

FIGURE 5–11. Jonathan's comic book–inspired illustrations.

Using a Pop-Up Book

Pop-up books can help children see spatial reality. I once showed six six-year-olds Damian Johnston's (1992) pop-up panorama of a rain forest, which captures the dense layerings of vegetation and the animals and insects who live in them. There is depth, but it is not the real depth of the natural objects; it is a compromise, but a valuable one.

Each member of the group was to produce a two-page text-illustration spread for a twelve-page concertina book. I placed the Johnston pop-up book on the edge of the table so that everyone could see it. After we had identified the animals and insects, the children selected a bright red parrot sitting in a tree as their main character and named him Peter.

Clockwise around the group, each pupil made his or her contribution in sequential order. Hayley started with, "A long time ago in the rain forest lived a parrot called Peter," followed by Neil's "When he was flying over the rain forest one day he saw a glowing torch." As the story unfolded, I wrote the dictated text on separate strips of paper. When someone was stuck for an idea, the others made suggestions.

At the end I read the entire story through. Since the children felt some parts didn't sequence well, they did some rewriting. I had already prepared

They were riding along the road one day.

FIGURE 5–12. Petri's galloping horses.

six pieces of tinted paper about a quarter of an inch smaller than the book pages to use for the illustrations. (I chose to use colored rather than white paper because I felt the colors would provide an approriate background mood.)

Their drawings were tentative at first: a flamingo here, a plant or tree shape there. The advantage of the rain forest pictorially is its sheer density. The children could conceive their illustrations like rows of vertical shelves with different items on each shelf.

We only had an hour and a half in which to work on the project, so at the same time the illustrations were emerging, the children in turn wrote their section of the narrative into the book. I felt it was important to finish in the allotted time. The challenge of "making a book by playtime" creates a sense of urgency, which can be electrifying.

Building People in Pieces

A drawing game can help children plan and enrich their illustrations. Give each student a sheet of eight-and-a-half-by-eleven paper—in the UK, A4 duplicating paper—(it can be smaller, but should have the same proportion of width to height) and tell them to use it in the portrait position. Draw a large-scale version of the paper on the chalkboard. Then have your students follow these instructions while you execute them on the chalkboard (the numbers in the example in Figure 5–13 correspond to the stages of the drawing as presented below). Children's attention spans vary considerably, so use your judgment about when to move to the next stage.

1. Draw an egg shape in the center top quarter of the area. Draw a central horizontal line through the egg. Below this line is the face, above this line, the hair/headgear of the figure. Draw in simple facial features—eyes, nose, lips, ears. What additional features (eye glasses, earrings, beard, freckles) can be added? Is the person male or female,

FIGURE 5–13. The basic layout for drawing a figure in a setting. The numbers correspond to the drawing stages.

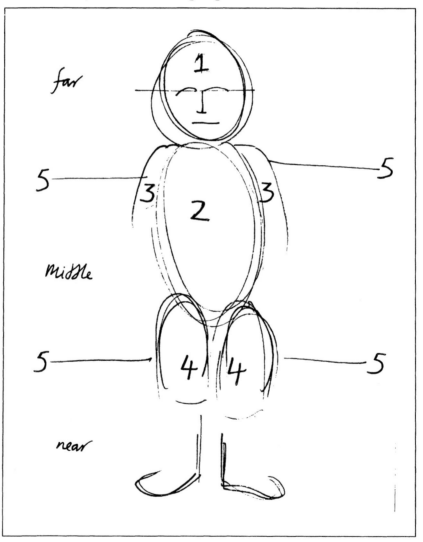

young or old? What kind of hairstyle does he or she have (bangs, ponytail, pigtails, braids, plaits, crew cut, long flowing hair, Afro, bald)? Is he or she wearing a hat (baseball cap, cowboy hat, crash helmet, straw hat, a hat decorated with flowers or fruit)?

2. Draw a sausage shape in the center of the area. (Be sure this is in a more or less dominant central position.)

3. Rough out the shoulder angles. Keep them fairly vague so they can be modified to become a dress, blouse, jacket, coat, T-shirt, etc. What is the person wearing? Does it match the kind of headgear drawn earlier? Is she in her best dress? Is he wearing work clothes? Is he or she dressed casually? When drawing clothing, remember things like lapels, necklines, belts, and pockets. Move on to the surface texture/pattern of the garments. Is it a flowered dress or shirt? If the person is wearing layered garments—a vest over a blouse, a scarf over a coat—might each have a different pattern or design?

4. Work on the final part of the figure, the area from the hips/waist to the feet. Draw in two thinner sausages to represent the legs. Extend the costume down to the feet. Since the concept of the figure is now more developed, this stage is more intuitive than the earlier stages and can take many forms—legs beneath a dress, jeans, creased trousers, Bermuda shorts; hiking boots, sneakers, high-heeled shoes, bare feet. Some pupils will have drawn the sections in a rationally organized way—a boy in a T-shirt, jeans, and sneakers, for example. Others will have produced a more complex or surreal figure— perhaps a girl wearing a tall hat, a brightly patterned vest, shorts, and swimming flippers. What the hands are holding (if anything)—a bag, a tennis racket, a telescope, a ball—is also important. Describe your character. Does he or she have a name yet? Is there a story in the making?

5. Since the central vertical area of the sheet of paper is now dominated by the character, turn to the setting. Where is the character standing? If it's outdoors, draw two horizontal lines on each side of the figure, one a third down from the top edge, the other a third up from the bottom edge, to delineate the foreground, middle ground, and background. Then fill in the bottom left and right panels—a city sidewalk, a field of corn, a garden path, a bridge over a stream. The foreground chosen will suggest the middle ground: city sidewalk, shops; field of corn, farm building; garden path, garden shed. The top panels inevitably portray the sky, which can be made more interesting

by including objects (buildings, trees) in the skyline. Has a hot-air balloon gotten stuck in a tree? Is a rocket coming down to earth? Is this where the story *really* starts? The simplest way to render an interior setting for the figure is to have two rather than three spatial depths. The foreground remains the area where the character is standing—carpet, a tiled floor littered with toys. The middle ground an background merge into one—the far wall of the room, perhaps including a doorway or a window, maybe a picture on wall, a bookshelf holding books and ornaments.

Figure 5–14 is a drawing produced as a result of this exercise.

Dress Me as You Please

A game similar to Building People in Pieces can be combined with it. As the figure emerges a plot takes shape around it. Each drawn detail adds new information.

Stand in front of the class and ask them to imagine you dressed for a particular occupation—a window cleaner, a postman, a deep-sea diver. (Children find the freedom to change the sex of the model particularly appealing. When I play this game, my students hoot when I tell them they can draw me—a bald middle-aged man—as a young woman with long golden hair if they choose.) A good technique is to radiate your pose slightly from left to right so that all the children can see you clearly and to keep up a running monologue:

> *I'm going to stand still like this for the next ten minutes. First, make an egg shape in the middle of the page near the top. That will be my head. Now make a long box shape under my head. That will be my body. Draw very lightly because you are not going to draw me, but invent for yourself how you want me to look in your picture.*
>
> *Let's all start with my head. Who is going to draw a woman? Who is going to draw a man? Am I wearing a hat? Is it going to fit my head tightly? Is it big and floppy with flowers on it? Think about how to make my hair come from under the hat and down each side of my face. Now think about my face. Am I a man with a beard and moustache or a lady wearing eye glasses? Is my face happy or sad? Unless my hair is long, don't forget to include my ears. Look at my real ears to help you draw them.*
>
> *Now let's move to the body. Don't draw the dull and boring*

FIGURE 5–14. Eight-year-old Omamah's drawing of Mrs. Smiley Face on a shopping spree.

shirt and tie I'm wearing. Make it something more colorful than that. If it is a woman you are drawing, how about a skirt and blouse or a dress? What kind of a pattern does the material have? Zigzags? Polka dots?

After drawing the figure, move on to the setting. Talk about possibilities: in a swimming pool, in a space rocket, in a secret underground city, on an airplane. This exercise can be used even with very young children. Figure 5–15 is a drawing produced by six-year-old Melanie.

Life Drawing

Having children pose for each other is an excellent way for them to learn body configurations and the way clothes drape. It is a natural progression from the piecemeal drawing games described above.

Eight-year-old Ali's illustrations in Figure 5–16 were drawn in this way, and they became the focus of a story about a boy who runs away from home.

FIGURE 5–15. Six-year-old Melanie's drawing of Mrs. Stripe.

One day mrs Stripe was going home from church. She had bort a lolly. the lolly was red. Mrs Stripe lived in the matins it was Very hot in the mountins mrs Stripe had two children there names were Betty and Ben When mrs stripe got home Betty and Ben were waching the T.V. mrs Stripe Sat down and suked her lolly then She told Betty and Ben

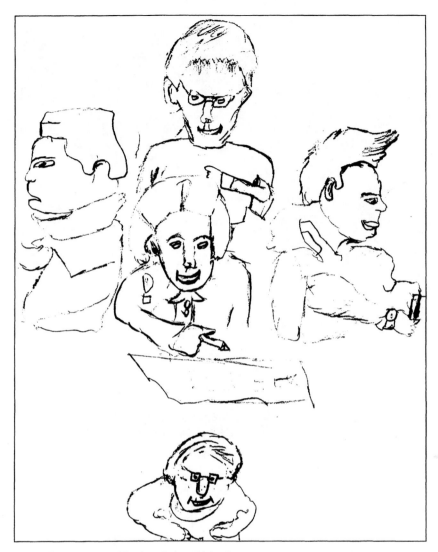

FIGURE 5–16. Ali's life drawings of his classmates.

Collecting and Using Visual Resources

Professional illustrators keep a file of visual resources (photographs from magazines, for example). They never know when they might be required to draw a buffalo or the Sydney Opera House as part of a book illustration. Collections of pictures from magazines let young book artists enhance the quality of their illustrations. Dominic, age ten, based one of his illustrations on a picture of a Victorian railroad car compartment (see Figure 5–17).

FIGURE 5–17. Dominic uses a picture from a magazine as a resource.

Then Bill said "Let's forge a painting." So they went to an art gallery and saw a Van Gogh.

4

Erdays they worked on copying Van Gogh's painting of his bedroom. It was AWFUL!!!

5

FIGURE 5–18. John's version of a Van Gogh.

Reproductions of famous pictures are also often used as resources. Nine-year-old John used Van Gogh's *Bedroom at Arles* as the basis of an illustration in his humorous story *The Forged Painting* (see Figure 5–18).

"Dutch Door" Books

A way for children to widen their repertoire of costume design for illustration is to have them make a "Dutch door" book, in which they draw various figures on pages split in half horizontally, so that each figure divides at the waist. Turning the tops or bottoms of pages creates different combinations of clothes and people. Figure 5–19 shows a number of examples from nine-year-old Robin's book, *Funny People*.

FIGURE 5–19. Robin's "Funny People."

Here's how to make a "Dutch door" book (the numbers in the diagram in Figure 5–20 are keyed to the instructions below):

1. Fold along the horizontal center line of a sheet of paper (landscape orientation).
2. Fold the left and right sides to the center.
3. Reopen the sheet, and cut the side panels at horizontal crease.
4. Fold in half as in step 1 and cut halfway through all side panels.
5. Fold side panels to the center and mark left and right waist positions on all cut panels.

You now have two sets of triple panels next to each other. The first two panels on each side have two movable parts, the innermost panels are undivided. (The children will draw only on the front of the panels.)

FIGURE 5–20. How to make a "Dutch door" book.

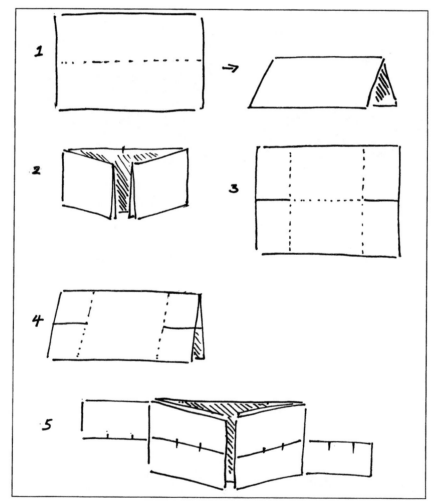

Here are some guidelines you can give your students:

- Make the left figures male and the right figures female, or use a mixture of both sexes on each side.
- Make the costume different on each half of each panel. For example: the top of panel 1 could be a clown with red nose and polka-dot bowler hat; the top of panel 2, a lady with headscarf, glasses, short coat, and neck scarf; the top of panel 3, an old sea captain with beard, cap, and high-necked sweater; the bottom of panel 1, brightly colored and patterned jeans with high-heeled shoes; the bottom of panel 2, a buckled tartan skirt with knee-length boots; the bottom of panel 3, shorts, thick socks, and hiking boots.
- Draw the arms in different positions. Give the hands objects to hold that are relevant to the type of person. (In the illustrations from Robin's book, the diver carries a spear, the weight lifter, dumbbells.)
- Small things, like a lapel badge or a scar on the face, can make statements about a character.
- Accessories, like handbags or jewelry, and the way they are worn communicate a great deal about a person.

Several published books use this "Dutch door" technique. My favorite is *Making Faces* by Norman Messenger (1992). Only the head and neck of the various characters are shown, divided into five parts. The left side of the page is a profile view, the right side, a front view. Figure 5–21 shows four of the faces constructed in ten-year-old Adam's homage to Messenger's book. These composites suggested a whole new spectrum of character possibilities to Adam and resulted in a story about a punk character called Florence.

Movable People

I've already mentioned how difficult it is to draw people in motion and pointed out that side views of figures indicate action better than front views (by the way, the greater the angle and proliferation of angles from the vertical, the faster the movement appears to be).

A very practical way to understand the complexities of body movement is for children to make a jointed figure in thick paper (or cardboard) held together by paper fasteners. This figure can then be arranged into any walking, running, jumping, sitting, or lying position.

A pattern of very basic shapes is included in Figure 5–22. (Keeping the shapes basic lets the children decide for themselves the sex, type, age, and other characteristics of the figures they draw using the model.) Cut the body parts out of thick paper or cardboard (make two sets of the arm, leg,

FIGURE 5–21. *Composite faces created from movable panels.*

and hand sections). Make holes at the points marked with crosses, and join limbs using "press-through" paper fasteners. (A completed figure is shown in Figure 5–23.)

Whenever a student requires a figure in a particular position, or wants to explore different poses and movements, he or she can use this paper figure as a guide. Ten-year-old Daisy, for example, used a movable paper figure to create the illustration shown in Figure 5–24.

By using these jointed figures, children will begin to recognize that a subtle movement of the head or an arm can convey nuances of meaning. A slightly bent head can imply contemplation. Hands raised to the bent head suggest remorse or anguished concern. Arms outstretched in front of the body say *Come to me*. Arms outstretched upward can give the impression of joy or terror depending on their position. There are thousands of ways we communicate feeling using the head and arms.

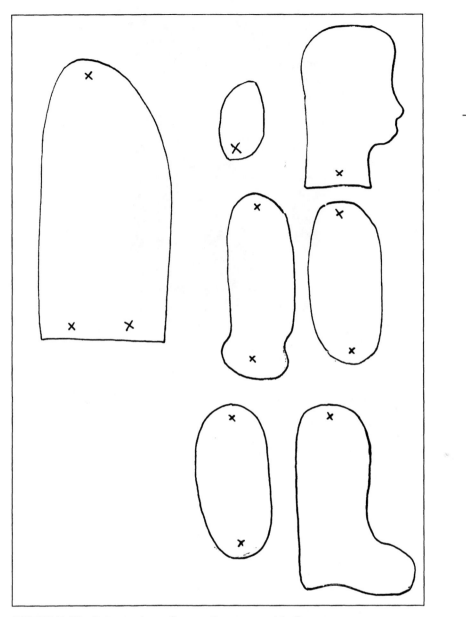

FIGURE 5–22. Pattern pieces for creating a movable figure.

The I-Can't-Draw Syndrome

As children get older, many of them become insecure about their ability to draw and their efforts often appear fussy and labored. They begin to depend on the ruler and the eraser. It's little wonder their illustrations in their books often fall well below the standard of their writing.

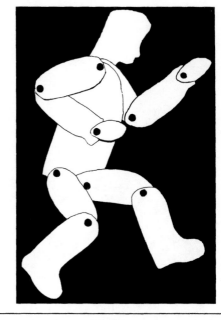

FIGURE 5–23. A completed movable figure.

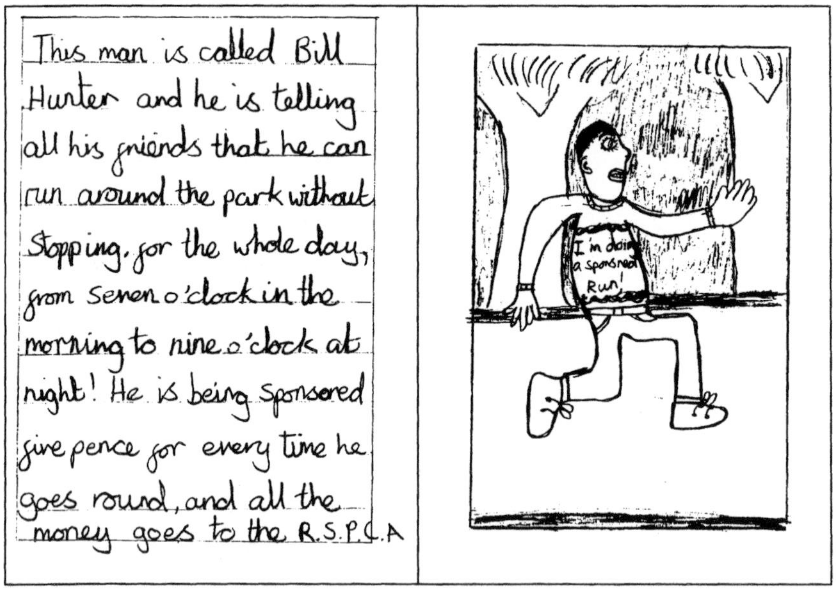

This man is called Bill Hunter and he is telling all his friends that he can run around the park without stopping, for the whole day, from seven o'clock in the morning to nine o'clock at night! He is being sponsored five pence for every time he goes round, and all the money goes to the R.S.P.C.A
I'm doin
a sponsred
Run!

FIGURE 5–24. Daisy's illustration drawn using a movable paper figure as a model.

A danger at this time is that children will take solace in stereotyped cartoon-style drawing. While cartoon imagery can teach a lot about movement in the human form and about the subtleties of facial expression, it's important that students adapt these influences into their own personal drawing style.

With increased experience, pupils will be able to use the structural techniques without needing the mechanical model. Joshua's drawings of cats in Figure 5–25 were created by laying down a framework of interlocking sausage and oval shapes and then drawing body, leg, and head features over them.

Pictures Without Words

The challenge of wordless picture stories is to make the illustrations move logically from one to the next; there must be no uncertainty about what is happening. Without words to fall back on to give vital information, the illustrations must convey the complete narrative.

A recurrent difficulty with telling a story through a set number of pictures is spacing out the episodes so that the whole story has a definite

FIGURE 5–25. Joshua's cat sketches.

FIGURE 5–26. Nine-year-old Amy's wordless picture story, *Jennifer's Lolly*.

FIGURE 5–27. Sarah's free interpretation of a Ray and Connie Burrows book.

"shape." In the example in Figure 5–26 Amy has twelve boxes in which to tell her story, and she develops it very nicely. The first four boxes show Jennifer preparing to go out shopping. In the middle section she buys a lollipop. Slowly the lollipop starts to grow, until it has grown so large that it floats upward, lifting Jennifer into the sky. The final box shows the lollipop delivering Jennifer safely home. The first six boxes prepare the viewer for the first high point of the plot—the lollipop's growing larger. The final four boxes depict the satisfying resolution—Jennifer's being lifted by the lollipop and carried home.

Philippe Dupasquier has made the wordless picture book into a fine art. Reading his *I Can't Sleep* (1990), one is not conscious that words are absent; indeed, the illustrations carry the narrative so well that words would seem an intrusion.

Learning from the Professionals

Children love looking at favorite picture books and recognizing favorite characters. Barbara Jordan (1992) notes how children identify very closely with the main characters in the fiction they read. This can, and often does, lead to the child's producing a narrative using those same characters and attempting to draw them. Nine-year-old Sarah's text and illustration in Figure 5–27 were prompted by Ray and Connie Burrows's *Baboushka*.

Much can be learned about design this way, providing the student can absorb an artist's style into her or his own expressive language.

Children learn to illustrate, as they learn to do most things, by progressing through developmental stages of understanding; they learn to draw by drawing, to make pictures by composing pictures. Examining book illustrations can only go part of the way to helping children understand how to make one themselves, however. We want our students to invest in their own innate talent.

6

Drawing Story Settings[*]

ENVISIONING SPACE AROUND PEOPLE

As the child builds up experience and practice in the confident use of a variety of tools and materials, his response to his personal environment is more readily interpreted into line, shape, form, pattern, and texture. The ability to interpret line, analyse shape, experience form, and match colour becomes apparent; proportion and depth are clearly problems to which he is beginning to apply his mind.   —MARGARET MORGAN

What does a lion look like? Children are always asking questions like this when they are working on an illustration. Usually, they find a picture of a lion in a reference book on animals, but then another problem arises: *I want it running toward me, not like it is in the photograph, lying down.*

Dilemmas like these show that there is no one objective "likeness" of anything; every object is perceived in relation to the viewer. Although children's early drawings show no distinction between flat and dimensional, they nevertheless use an uncanny logic to express space in drawing.

I am indebted to Rudolf Arnheim's seminal Art and Visual Perception *(1974), which has informed much of the material in this chapter.*

FIGURE 6–1. Various interpretations of a line.

FIGURE 6–2. Gregory's illustration of Father Christmas.

Plane

Looking at a picture is like looking through one surface of a cube to its opposite end. Everything in the picture's environment appears to recede from the viewer, and only one plane of an object is visible at any one time. Children use a range of techniques to represent this phenomenon.

Space

A single line on a piece of paper cannot be seen as itself alone; it always relates to the two-dimensional space around it. The imagined content of this empty environment conditions the way the line is perceived. It can't be seen as lying in a flat plane but rather as being in front of or within a "ground." In the interpretations of a line in Figure 6–1, it is perceived as a path, a bed, a railroad track, the boundary of a playground, the edge of a desk, a wall, a swimming pool, and the horizon.

The base-line orientation

The top/bottom, left/right focus of the drawing can either be vertical (people, houses, trees) or horizontal (gardens, streets, tabletops). The dominant figures in five-year-old Gregory's illustration in Figure 6–2 (Santa Claus and the fireplace) are seen as objects in vertical space, the area around them as the receding depth of horizontal space. Santa Claus and the cat rest on an imaginary line—a platform at the bottom of the frame.

Children impose order on their pictures by defining this ground line. This is the stage on which the main action takes place. The other edges of

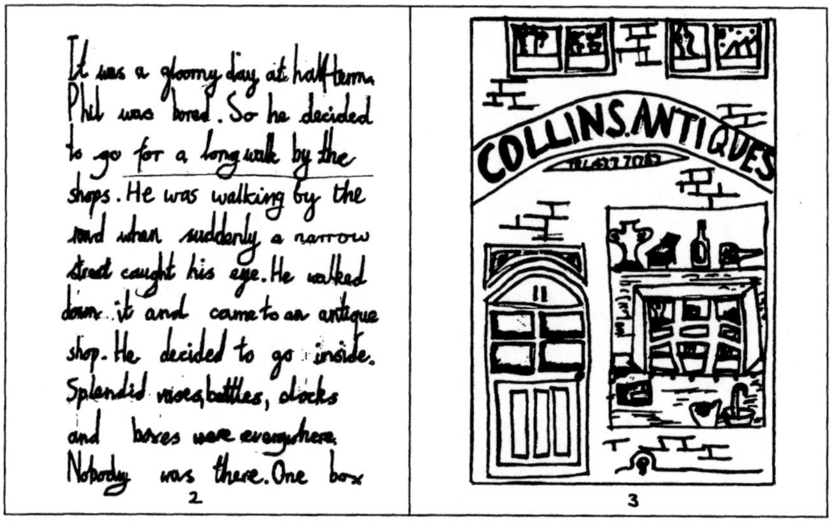

FIGURE 6–3. Edward's detailed illustration of the front of an antiques shop.

FIGURE 6–4. An illustration from John's book, *The Time Machine*.

the frame are the boundaries of the proscenium. Looking at a book illustration is like sitting in a theatre, like looking through a window either into an interior, or out to an exterior. The actor and the stage (the figure and the ground) are essential to the illustration.

People (or animals or objects with human qualities) in book illustrations command our attention more than anything else because we expect them to be the subject of the story. If they are not present, the eye searches for something that it can identify as the main subject.

Ten-year-old Edward's book *The Magic Antique Box* is unusual in that nowhere does the main character, Phil, appear in the illustrations. (Satoshi

Its no use said teddy
Iv got an idea said the doll
the dolls and teddy went home
and woke up Jane couldnt
belive wat was happening but
she agreeded to go with
them she gotout a torch and
put on her dressing gown
they went out soon they
found the cat and began
the long walk home they
had a lovely easter day
and lived happily ever after

the end

FIGURE 6–5. Eve's illustration from her story, *The Toys That Came Alive*.

Kitamura does something similar with the main character in *UFO Diary*.) The shop front that fills the first illustration panel (see Figure 6–3) holds our attention with its detail and, in our mind's eye, we see the protagonist enter it.

However, there are exceptions to this general rule. Sometimes the eye-catching imagery of the stage holds our attention more than the figure. In eight-year-old John's illustration in Figure 6–4, for example, the underground kingdom and volcanoes are more visually enticing than the main character.

The figure

Stories are built around a main character. In depicting the interaction of characters, one of them needs to dominate. If we are unclear who this person is we feel confused. Six-year-old Eve's composition in Figure 6–5 is satisfying because we focus first on the dominant figure of Jane holding the teddy bear on the left and then move to the smaller cat and two dolls on the right.

Isometric projection

The graphic art of Japan is often cited as exemplifying *isometric projection*. In this drawing technique, objects acquire depth through obliqueness, but the size of the receding object is constant throughout. Helen's street scene in Figure 6–6 is drawn at a nonreceding oblique angle, the house fronts shown at right angles to the street. It is characteristic for children to pass through this mode of drawing before progressing to simple one-point perspective in which distant objects taper away from the viewer toward a single vanishing point.

By five or six years of age children use size to differentiate people and objects that are nearby and farther away. In six-year-old Joanne's illustration in Figure 6–7, the giant (the main character) is near to us, the tiger (the secondary character) is set slightly further back, and the rest of the animals (minor characters) are farthest away.

By age seven or eight, children begin placing more distant objects higher on the page. In Jessica's illustration in Figure 6–8, her base-line figure dominates the bottom half of the panel, houses occupy the upper middle area, and distant hills are placed at the top.

Perhaps the biggest challenge of all in picture making is realizing that in order to depict a three-dimensional object realistically one must trans-

FIGURE 6–6. Seven-year-old Helen's use of isometric projection.

wasnt · He was a good Gi ant. One nigt he Frigtend away all the Ghosts so the forest was much more quiet And so for a week it was quiet until the Giant came back.

FIGURE 6–7. The characters' size as cues to their proximity and importance.

late it into a two-dimensional configuration of lines and shapes. This of course only happens gradually.

"X-ray" pictures

Children's drawings of interior scenes are often superimposed on a two-dimensional representation of the exterior structure. The square stands for cubic space. (See Figures 6–9 and 6–10 for examples.) It's ironic that while we accept that the television screen often represents a demolished wall of a room, we regard these "see-through" drawings as naïve!

FIGURE 6–8. Jessica's top-to-bottom positioning to indicate depth.

He took her to his house under the sea And watched dolphin T-V

FIGURE 6–9. Six-year-old Michelle shows a dolphin and Aunt Mabel inside the dolphin's house watching dolphin TV.

FIGURE 6–10. Ten-year-old Adam uses the "X-ray" strategy over the whole spatial field to encompass as much information as possible (notice the distant lunar landscape).

FIGURE 6–11. A ten-year-old's use of foreshortening.

FIGURE 6–12. An illustration from Alex's *The Adventures of Wizard Q.*

FIGURE 6–13. Ten-year-old Fareed's illustration from *George's Jeans.*

Foreshortening

Both the isometric and perspective methods of drawing use two-dimensional lines and shapes to represent three-dimensional objects. *Foreshortening* is a visual cue that parts of an object lie at different distances from the observer. The forearm and hand in ten-year-old Eric's drawing in Figure 6–11, projecting forward from the torso, have been drawn foreshortened.

Overlapping

Overlapping is unavoidable in drawing because objects block one another everywhere. The simplest way of presenting a figure is a "flat" frontal drawing, but as soon as statements are made about the figure in animation, intricate crossings of limbs are necessary. Ten-year-old Alex's drawing of an arm in front of a figure in three-quarter profile (see Figure 6–12) is a sophisticated example.

When students draw background objects "around" foreground figures (see Figure 6–13), they have reached a stage of abstract thought. One must be able to imagine the object behind the figures to draw the parts of it that are visible.

Figure Placement

Where figures are placed in a picture is of enormous significance. There is a dynamic direction from left to right in pictures. Alex's Wizard in

FIGURE 6–14. The characters in this illustration appear to be returning from rather than going somewhere.

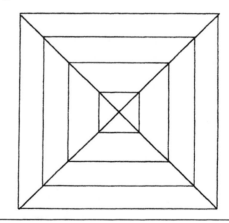

FIGURE 6–15. Symmetrical points in a structural frame.

Figure 6–12 is moving in a rightward direction, looking to the next page.

An object at the right side of a picture has more weight. When two objects of equal size are placed left and right, the one on the right looks larger. To compensate for this, the one on the left side has to be drawn larger or appear more significant in some other way. The eye moves from a place of initial attention on the left to an ultimate focus on the right. "Reading" a picture from left to right makes the movement look easier; movement in the opposite direction appears to be pushing against the current (see Figure 6–14).

FIGURE 6–16. Eight-year-old Michala's illustration from her story, *Dirty Dan and the Mysterious Bundle*.

Structural symmetry

A picture's design is not only conditioned by its boundaries, but also by the receding vertical and horizontal axes and by the diagonals (see Figure 6–15). Every object in a picture is seen as having a location.

Interacting forms situated at an equal distance from the center of the frame (see Figure 6–16) suggest stability. If the interacting forms are

FIGURE 6–17. Nine-year-old Jason's illustration from his story, *The Pet Dog.*

FIGURE 6–18. An illustration from Mary and John's *The Baby Dinosaur.*

moved to one side, as in Figure 6–17, they look as if they have slipped out of place. The large empty center of Mary and John's illustration from *The Baby Dinosaur* (see Figure 6–18) gives the impression that something is missing.

An off-center character in a frame appears to have slipped from the middle or to want to move away even further. The psychological structure of a picture is a play of attraction and repulsion, an interplay of directed tensions.

Visual dynamics

A picture book would be boring if all the main objects in the illustrations were placed symmetrically. The eye demands variety. Dynamic movement is more compelling than static forms, exaggeration more persuasive than conventional shapes. Diagonal lines make a composition more spirited than vertical and horizontal ones.

Equilibrium is attained when forces within the picture compensate for one another. The vertical figure of the cat on the left of Laura's composition (Figure 6–19) is balanced asymmetrically by the horizontal

FIGURE 6–19. Nine-year-old Laura's illustration from *The Cat and the Whale.*

FIGURE 6–20. Ten-year-old Sarah's illustration from *Flower Power.*

whale on the right. In Figure 6–20 Sarah's solid architectural structure of verticals and horizontals is energized by a profusion of diagonals—the nailed wooden planks, the signs, the figure's arm and leg, the broken window panes, and the stars. (Perhaps Sarah has produced almost too much energy here!) The dominant oblique angles of Ammar's footballer in Figure 6–21 are counterbalanced by the vertical thrust of the ball into the air.

An unbalanced composition looks ambiguous. We need to be certain about the structural placing of shapes in a picture: is it symmetrical or asymmetrical? The eye is confused if it cannot tell what the pattern is trying to say.

Weight

The character or mood of a picture is largely responsible for its *weight.* Weight can be achieved and balanced in many ways. The multitude of minor figures on the left of Mahbubul's illustration for *The Magician* (see Figure 6–22) is balanced by the one dominant figure on the right.

Size and *color* also affect weight. Red is heavier than blue, bright

FIGURE 6–21. Ten-year-old Ammar's illustration from *Up United!*

FIGURE 6–22. Eleven-year-old Mahbubul's illustration from *The Magician.*

colors are heavier than dark ones. A full-frame face gives the impression that the character is very near to us. In Figure 6–23, Adam highlights Mrs. Thigmire's ebullient personality by filling the frame with her portrait.

Special interest also affects balance, so that a small but precious or

FIGURE 6–23. Ten-year-old Adam's full-face illustration of Mrs. Space Thigmire.

FIGURE 6–24. Ten-year-old Rebecca's illustration from her story, *Mr. Attaché*.

interesting object will have more weight than its physical size. The odd-looking object the character in Figure 6–24 is holding is relatively small, but it has weight because it raises our curiosity.

Similarly, what might be called *personal interest* (for example, the observer's wishes or fears) influences the weight in a picture; desirable or frightening objects appear to be larger than they are.

Finally, a higher-placed object appears to have more weight than a lower-placed one, although in the world around us there are more things lower down than higher up. (Book designers customarily leave more space at the bottom than at the top of a page.)

"Lists"

As the dividing line between fact and fiction has become more blurred in children's publishing, the illustration techniques of information books have crossed over into storybooks. In Figure 6–25, nine-year-old Rosie has drawn the characters and main objects in her story not as an integrated picture but as isolated images, like a visual list in a reference book.

FIGURE 6–25. The illustration as list.

Depth

At first, children represent the bottom edge of the picture—the base line—as the earth's surface; the top edge as the skyline; and the large middle section as where the character is or where events take place. Gradually, as they learn the art of representing three dimensions through two-dimensional illusion, they perceive what is nearest as *foreground*; what is farthest away as *background*; and the space in between the two as *middle ground*. We saw in

Chapter 4 how quite young children can be helped to think in this spatial way.

Of course, it is impossible to say where one ground becomes the next in what is the representation of an unbroken vista to infinity. The "depth" of the picture plane, that imaginary space between where the picture begins and where it ends, and the distances covered by concepts like *near*, *middle*, and *distant* can vary considerably.

The picture plane can be divided into variable "thicknesses." These can be moved up and down within the picture area to give emphasis to the near, middle or distant ground. In the first of the examples in Figure 6–26, the foreground window interior dominates the composition; in the second, the middle-distance house monopolizes the scene; and in the third the background mountain landscape almost fills the picture area.

Understanding Space by Using Folded Paper

Layering cut and folded paper can help children perceive the intricacies of space in illustration. Below are two techniques you may find helpful.

Technique 1

1. Crease a piece of eight-and-a-half-by-eleven paper—or A4 duplicating paper—(landscape orientation) into four equal vertical folds.

FIGURE 6–26. Examples of illustrations dominating the foreground, middle ground, and background.

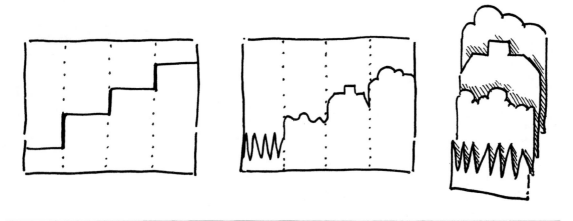

FIGURE 6–27. Diagram for folding technique 1.

2. Lightly draw steps on the four folds (see Figure 6–27a).
3. Then vary the shape in some way so that each of the four steps has different contours (see Figure 6–27b) and cut away the paper above each contour.
4. Refold the paper and see what the spatial composition suggests (see Figure 6–27c).

Folded down flat, the form gives four successive areas of depth to the picture plane—foreground, near middle ground, far middle ground, and background (see Figure 6–28). How one interprets these areas is a matter of choice. The two middle layers can be interpreted as occupying a dominant middle ground, but one of these can be shifted down, giving dominance to the foreground, or up, accenting the background. As a rule, interior depth tends to be much shorter than exterior depth and allows for more refined incremental details.

Technique 2

A possible problem with the zigzag technique above is that the alternating opening out of the sections can be confusing. Here is another paper-folding and -cutting strategy in which all the sections hinge on the same side.

1. Crease an eight-and-a-half-by-eleven piece of paper—or A4 duplicating paper—(landscape orientation) on the vertical and cut panels as shown in Figure 6–29a.

FIGURE 6–28. Sarah's layered illustrations.

2. Fold panel 3 over panel 5, and panel 2 under panels 4 and 5 (see Figure 6–29b).
3. Fold panel 4 over to the left and panel 1 under to the right (see Figure 6–29c).
4. Fold panel 4 under panels 1 and 2, and panel 1 over to the left (see Figure 6–29d).
5. Finally fold panel 1 under panel 4 (see Figure 6–29e).

(When artwork is complete, the back of panel 1 can be glued to a base if desired).

Now you (or you students) need to draw the various levels of a scene: for example, a gate and fence in the foreground; a garden in the near middle ground; a shop in the far middle ground; and a railroad scene in the far distance at the top of the page (see Figure 6–30). By pushing the far distance to the top of the picture area, the fore- and middle ground are opened up to view. In an illustration context, it is a way of making pictures narratively exciting. Each spatial layer comprises a location.

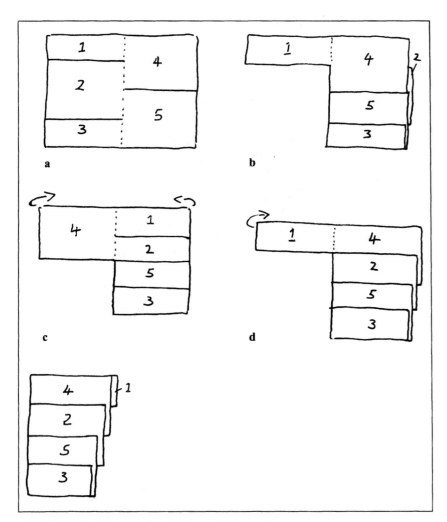

FIGURE 6–29. Diagram for folding technique 2.

The cutting away of areas between forms reveals what is beneath in the next layer.

Drawing Interiors

The inside of a cathedral can provide the artist with as much depth as an exterior scene. However, conventional interiors like a living room or a kitchen have relatively short spatial depth—a character is usually seen sitting or standing in front of the rear wall of the room. In Figure 6–31, the foreground is taken up by the inventor's worktable; the rest of the vertical

FIGURE 6–30. Ten-year-old Caity's folded-paper illustration, *The Hat Shop*.

area of the picture comprises the background wall, which is made interesting by shelves of bottles.

As we shall see in the next chapter, drawing tables, chairs, and cupboards in perspective is a challenge to the young illustrator, so objects in interiors are often drawn as head-on, thus avoiding the necessity of receding oblique lines.

FIGURE 6–31. Ten-year-old Jim's illustration for his story, *Dr. Deedson's Inventions*.

Decorative Interiors

There is much to draw in the interior of a really interesting room, as can be seen from so many excellently designed children's picture books. An

FIGURE 6–32. Seven-year-old Harry's illustration, *The King of the Amazons.*

awareness-raising game is to improvise a room's interior with a class. Discuss the carpet on the floor and its pattern, cupboards and what they contain, decorative objects like vases on the cupboard, the wallpaper design, and things hanging on the wall.

Van Gogh loved placing his portrait subjects against richly textured wallpapers, just as over a century earlier, court artists placed the aristocracy against gold-embroidered canopies and drapes for their portraits. Pattern and texture play an important part in illustration. By cutting a head-and-shoulders contour and folding it in front of a background (see Figure 6–32), pupils can treat both the figure and the setting as quite separate design tasks. This can develop into conventional illustration in which both kinds of artwork are drawn on one surface.

Atmospheric Perspective

Whereas converging lines and overlapping forms help to plot the position of objects, atmospheric perspective describes the less tangible effects of light and climate on the visible world. Turn-of-the-century illustrators of children's books were very good at exploiting this: think, for example, of the wispy branches against starlit skies of Kay Nielson, and the enchanted and often sinister underworld depths of Arthur Rackham. And it is alive today in the impressionistic watercolor washes of Michael Foreman's illustrations in *One World* (1990).

In Figure 6–33, ten-year-old Natalie captures the mood of a moonlit wood. The main character of this story, David, is drawn quite small on the far left, while on the far right the personified moon takes up a sizable area. Natalie uses the whole of the two-page spread to increase the illusion of space. The light from David's small torch radiates out and over the page centerfold to its destination—the circle of the full moon. The spatial dynamics appear to expand the paper so that the pages seem much larger than they are. The darkness of the small hill on which David perches accents the wide empty space of the middle ground, which seems bathed with light from the torch.

Looking into Children's Illustrations

Understanding the form and structure of pictorial composition in general and the psychology of children's picture making in particular is essential to teaching illustration. It can help us understand why a child's illustration fails to "work." Betty Edwards (1989) makes the point that children have a natural sense of design in their pictures and that if a figure or object is removed, the composition looks wrong. This is undoubtedly true, but as they develop artistically their knowledge and experience with composition needs to be guided.

FIGURE 6–33. Ten-year-old Natalie's illustration for her story, *When the World Sleeps.*

We have seen that empty space in a picture can be a balancing feature or give the appearance of a hole, something missing. But the rules can be broken and a picture can still "work": other factors, like our relationship with the subject matter, can compensate for a structural inconsistency. So much of this is intuitive when we make pictures, yet to understand the mechanics of this built-in logic deepens our knowledge of how pictures elucidate a text. In time we learn to see that making a series of related illustrations can be as intricate and as intellectually demanding and fulfilling as writing a good story.

7

Perspectives on Illustrated Narratives

MAKING THINGS LOOK THE WAY THEY ARE

Perspective is . . . beautiful. For, once the basic principles have been learnt, you will find that it helps you to draw much more confidently, while also opening up a whole new field of exciting and previously unexpected subject matter. —ANGELA GAIR

At the beginning of an extended book-making project (it continued over a period of three years) with a group of nine- and ten-year-olds, I gave each student a blank concertina book and invited him or her to fill it with an illustrated story. We talked about layout possibilities, we looked at some published picture books, and then they went to work.

Steven created *The Space Ship*, a two-page spread from which is shown in Figure 7–1. Steven's narrative was initially written on strips of paper that he could place anywhere he chose on the page. Somewhat unusually, he selected the middle area. In this five-page book, Dan, the protagonist, walks through a wood and discovers a space ship. Once inside, he pushes the knobs on the control panel. The space ship takes off. He travels up into space, but before returning home he stops off on the moon and makes friends with aliens.

Steven's story is unoriginal, but it does have a rudimentary sequence, a "shape." Whether by design or accident, Steven has maintained the five narrative sections at roughly the same number of words, which gives a balanced appearance to the pages; because they are brief, there are generous spaces for the artwork.

However, the illustrations do little to enhance the text or feed the eye with inventive picture making. The first two illustrations are little more than a schematic spatial division of the page, a characteristic normally associated with younger pupils. The tree shapes seem to prop up the sky rather than stand in the middle distance with the sky as backdrop, and an ineffective Dan stands on the base line. Steven has not yet started to think in a spatial way.

A weak story idea impedes the development of both writing and illustration. Steven's drawings are lackluster partly because his experience with drawing is limited, but also because the content of his narrative feeds him so little information.

Figure 7–2 is a two-page spread from Gary's first concertina book. Common problems with perspective are evident. Objects are on a base line, except for the box and the ghost. This means that half the page is uneventful; it fails to hold the eye.

Steven's second book, *The Robber* (see Figure 7–3), was created imme-

FIGURE 7–1. Two pages from Steven's initial effort, *The Space Ship.*

diately after *The Space Ship*. Looking at them both, you would probably assume the second was done a year or two later than the first. In Gary's second book (see Figure 7–4) the active pictorial compositions not only invite the onlooker's attention, but encourage inquiries about Bill's identity and intention as he is about to enter the apartment above him. How did this development come about?

Setting the Scene

I used Colin McNaughton's picture book *Who's That Banging on the Ceiling?* (1992) as a primary example when I began working with the group.

McNaughton designed the book so that the pages are lifted rather than turned from right to left. This is not a gimmick, but a visual device that echoes the story setting, a multistory apartment building. Page 1, set on

FIGURE 7–2. A two-page spread from Gary's first concertina book, *The Haunted House*.

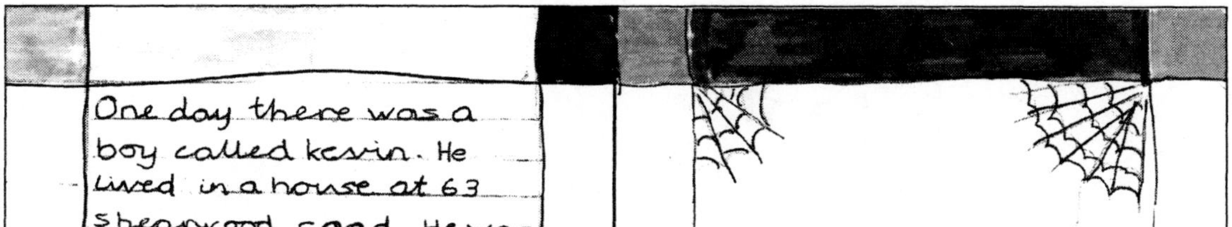

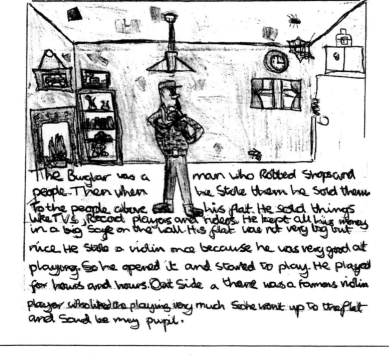

The Burglar was a man who Robbed shops and people. Then when he stole them he sold them to the people above his flat. He sold things like TVs, Record players and videos. He kept all his money in a big safe on the wall. His flat was not very big but nice. He stole a violin once because he was very good at playing. So he opened it and started to play. He played for hours and hours. Outside a there was a famous violin player who liked the playing very much. So he went up to the flat and said be my pupil.

FIGURE 7–3. Two pages from Steven's story, *The Robber*.

FIGURE 7–4. Two pages from Gary's second book, *The Music From Above*.

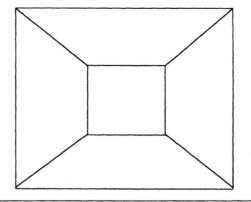

FIGURE 7–5. *Perspective of the interior of a cube.*

the ground floor, shows an irritated Mrs. Manky shaking her fists at the ceiling of her living room and the noise coming from the room above. The page above (set in the apartment above) reveals that the noise is caused by a dinosaur dancing the fandango. The remaining twenty-six pages continue this pattern of hilarious cause-and-effect goings-on upward through the floors. The climax of the story is a foldout section of four pages showing King Kong tap-dancing on the roof.

Shaping a Theme

I then distributed concertina books in which the pages flipped up (like a calendar) rather than turned, and asked my students to begin to think about a story that would reflect this vertical progression.

I also showed them a miniature violin and bow in a case and asked them to mold a character and story around it. Who was their character? What was his or her name? What were his or her circumstances? What did he or she wish to accomplish? What was his or her apartment like? Just as Mrs. Manky's apartment on the first page of McNaughton's book identifies her as a cat fanatic—there are cats and pictures of cats everywhere—could their illustrations reveal aspects of their character's interests, life style, and personal preferences?

Choosing a Page Layout

The period of character development is an essential prelude to the next stage, laying out the page design through which the story will develop. We

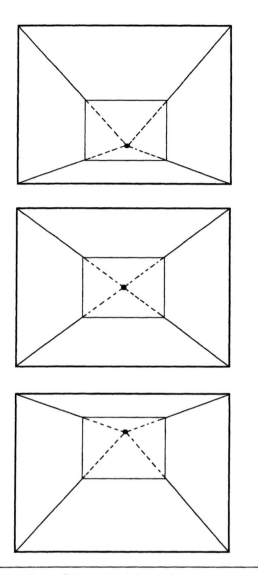

FIGURE 7–6. *Three views of one-point perspective.*

decided that the first page would be a full-page illustration whose visual imagery would establish a scenario.

On the first blank page I had each student lightly pencil in a perspective drawing of the interior of a cube (see Figure 7–5). Then we talked about one-point perspective (see Figure 7–6), in which the viewer stands in line with a single vanishing point, which can be placed outside or inside the picture area (the vanishing points in the three examples in Figure 7–6 are all within the picture area). By moving this horizon line from lower to higher, the viewer appears to be higher than, on the same level as, or below what is being drawn. Having this box as a prompt helps children draw objects and settings receding into spatial depth.

Steven (Figure 7–3) does this fairly well; the sides of the table recede in the direction of the vanishing point, as does the top of the fireplace. Gary (Figure 7–4) is less successful; he seems unable to grasp the perspective obliques—all the objects are drawn head-on (the TV seems to be levitating!).

(Of course, we are applying sophisticated scientific criteria to largely aesthetic concerns here. These children are learning a framework for making pictures that is satisfactory as far as it goes. This new way of seeing things has to be learned gradually, through trial and error; but we have to know that an error has been made, and why and how it can be corrected.)

Then I had one of the students model the toy violin in the playing position, and we discussed matters related to costume: printed and woven patterns on fabrics, the drape of clothes on the body in various positions, accessories like earrings and necklaces, right down to shoes and shoelaces. Pupils were encouraged to use these ideas rather than what the model was wearing.

Then I posed a final challenge: design a room with doors, windows, shelves, cupboards, wallpaper, books, pictures, boxes, vases, plants.

At the next session we concentrated on beginning the written narrative on the second page of the book, which could be either a whole page of writing or a half page of writing combined with a half-page illustration. Steven's main character is a thief who sells stolen goods to the people who live above him. Unfortunately, he virtually reproduces his first illustration in conjunction with his second-page text.

What Words Say, What Pictures Show

Scott is an above-average writer and illustrator who thinks instinctively in a book way; his book *Utopia* is shown in its entirety in Figure 7–7. On page 1, the main character, Hans Keller, is playing his violin. He discovers a key that, on page 2, carries him up by an "immense energy" to the balcony on top of the house (page 3). Here there is "a solid oak door surrounded by limestone," which Hans opens by inserting the key in the lock. The door opens onto a landscape. The next three pages depict a sequential journey through that landscape: on page 4, Hans is walking down a path through trees; further along (page 5) he crosses a bridge over a river; and

Hans Keller was
playing his violin
which was his pastime.
He was playing Beethavens
pastral symphany to his
dog called Fritz. Fritz was
fully engrossed when he heard
this music.
This particular day
Hans was distracted from his playing. He
had discovered a gilt Key on the top of his
book case. When he picked the key up an immense
energy drew him across the parlour, through
the passage and up the balcony to the top of
the house.

FIGURE 7–7. Part 1 of Scott's *Utopia*.

When Hans stepped out onto the balcony the image of a solid oak door surrounded by limestone carved with patterns appeared. The force attracting the key increased. It was drawn to a huge gold padlock on the door like a magnet.

The key left Hans grip and unlocked the doors which opened majestically to reveal a stupendous sight. Strong beams of sunlight streamed down through an avenue of tall poplar trees. A sweet scent wafted through the fresh air. A cobbled path invited Hans to follow it.

FIGURE 7–7b *continued*

A brightly coloured archaeopteryx swooped down from a tree towards Hans. To Hans's surprise it began to speak. "Follow me. I have been sent to be your guide throughout your visit to Utopia." He led Hans along the cobbled path towards a hill. Far in the distance Hans could see a tower on the top of the hill.

On the way to the tower Hans had to cross an arched stone bridge. He stopped to look into the crystal blue stream below. Tropical coloured fish leapt about in the stream. To Hans's amazament and delight some of the fish started to fly.

On either side of the path lay carpets of rainbow coloured flowers amongst lusclous green grass. Crimson poppies towered over shy little forget me nots. Golden daffodils swayed gently in the breeze. Regal purple orchids and smart pink fuschias painted a breath taking picture.

Hans reached the tower at the top of the hill. He discovered that the door was locked. The archaeopteryx flew towards him with the golden key in its beak. Was this Hans's destination or did another adventure await him behind the closed door.

FIGURE 7–7c continued

finally, he approaches a tower (page 6). These distant landscapes are enlarged, so that one examines in detail what is suggested on page 3. A mysterious flying creature is introduced along the way, and the tower and the creature serve as the ambivalent climax of the story, which is resolved in the continuation (see Figure 7–8), which Scott wrote and illustrated the following year.

In the space/time continuum, art is good at defining space but poor at suggesting time. With language, it is the other way round. In Scott's story, Hans progresses up the stairs to the balcony. Our imagination pictures this journey through time as we read the narrative, but the illustration can only record one moment of that journey—Hans halfway up the stairs. Words effectively describe historical data (for example, that playing the violin is Hans's pastime) and aural images (for example, that he is playing Beethoven's Pastoral Symphony.) Art is weak at both of these dimensions, but strong on defining the visual appearance of material situations. Reading or hearing a verbal description of a room's interior, we have to place, *by our own design*, the objects under discussion: "There was a picture on the wall" invites us to place the picture, arbitrarily, on the wall we have imagined. The strength of art is that the room, right down to the particulars of wallpaper design and light fixtures, can be represented in the "reality" of two-dimensional spatial illusion. Fusing pictures and language heightens expressive response and helps clears up uncertainties.

In the first part of *Utopia*, the areas of color and pencil lines that separate them are of similar tonal strength. The pictures are flat and lack sharpness; but ink line work can accentuate the essential form of objects. Continuous thick black edges around forms tend to deenergize them (they look like cutouts), so the art of line work is as much to do with the absence of line as with line itself. The pressure applied to a pen moderates the quality of the line; thus receding objects are drawn more lightly than dominant foreground ones.

In the hands of a professional these techniques looks easy, as in McNaughton's illustrations. (Incidentally, in *Who's That Banging* he uses ultramarine ink line work, and this pleasantly softens the textual quality of the forms.) In his continuation of *Utopia*, Scott uses a fine black felt-tipped pen. At first he uses it cautiously to highlight shapes, and he makes the common mistake of outlining nearly every drawn object (the clouds in the third illustration look particularly artificial by being drawn in this way), but by the last illustration (a room interior) he is holding the pen lightly (notice the grain of the floorboards). He is still

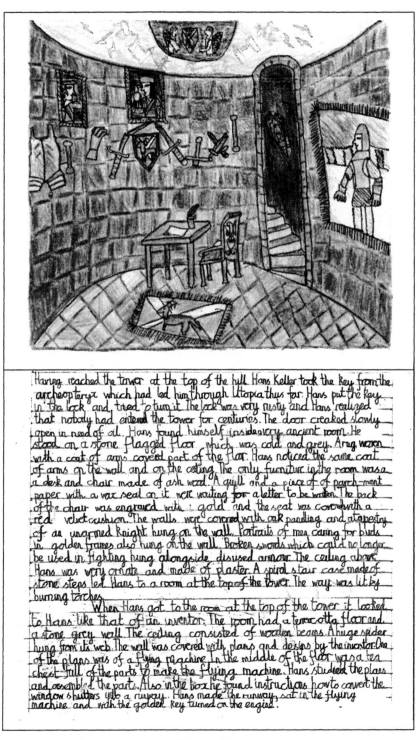

FIGURE 7–8. The continuation of Scott's *Utopia*.

FIGURE 7–8b *continued*

The propellor began to rotate and the flying machine took off up the runway and out of the tower window. The archaeopteryx led Hans out of the tower window. The archaeopteryx led Hans out of Utopia. Whilst over the sea a storm began. A vortex sucked Hans out of his flying machine. Hans felt dizzy as he spun around. Eventually the spinning stopped and Hans found himself back on the balcony of his house. He held the golden key in his hand.

Inspired by all he had experienced in Utopia Hans later wrote a violin concerto which he entitled Utopia. Utopia made him rich and famous. Hans refurbished his home in the style of Utopia and comissoned an artist to paint a picture of an archaeopteryx for him. Hans mounted the golden key to this picture as he felt it was symbolic as the key to his imagination and success.

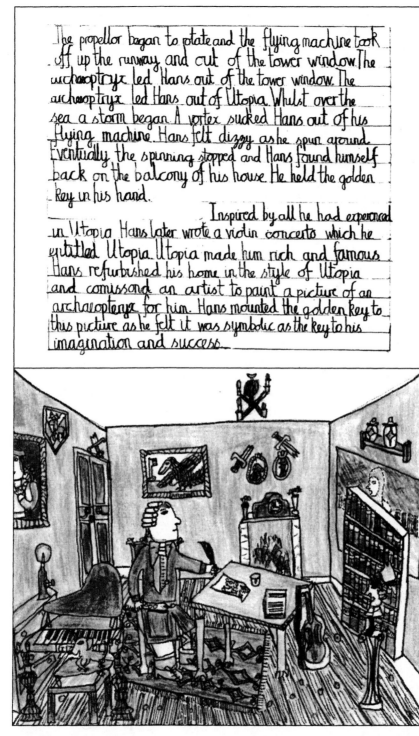

FIGURE 7–8c *continued*

struggling with linear perspective, although it is much improved since his earlier work.

The narrative in part 2 continues where part 1 ends:

> *Having reached the tower at the top of the hill, Hans Keller took the key from the archeopteryx which had led him through Utopia thus far. Hans put the key in the lock and tried to turn it. The lock was very rusty and Hans realized that nobody had entered the tower for centuries. . . .*

At the top of the tower is a room with terra-cotta floor tiles and a box full of parts to make a flying machine. Hans assembles it and makes a runway from the room's window shutters. He climbs into the aircraft and it takes off through the window. The third illustration shows the archaeoptryx leading the way through the clouds, but a vortex sucks Hans out of the plane and he lands back on the balcony of his house. In the top illustration Hans, reinstated in his house, prepares to write a violin concerto inspired by his experiences.

Perspective Studies

Scott's perspective studies shown in Figure 7–9, which he did in the third and final year I worked with this particular group of children, show how much more accurate his drawing of perspective is becoming. Both studies use the same vanishing point, one exterior and the other interior. Scott is finding that drawing the recession of doors and windows in a street of terraced houses is a particularly daunting challenge.

FIGURE 7–9. Scott's perspective studies.

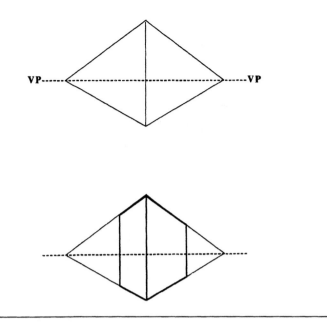

FIGURE 7–10. Two-point perspective.

Two-point perspective

In two-point perspective, which describes three-dimensionality better than one-point perspective, two receding parallel lines run toward their vanishing points on the horizon (see Figure 7–10). When children grasp these scientific principles of conveying space, they are entering the domain of the professional illustrator. It is an important step forward. By progressing to two-point perspective, children can include much more information in their pictures.

To introduce these students to two-point perspective, I distributed more six-fold concertina books and showed them how to divide them into two three-paneled "cinemascope" exterior scenes (see Figure 7–11). They drew a central vanishing point in the center page of each three-page area and added guidelines radiating outward to cover all three pages. In effect, the center page became a one-point perspective study that then extended left and right to vanishing points that lay outside the picture.

The theme of the first illustration was A Street as It Is Now, the second, The Same Street as It Becomes in the Future. Each illustration was to be held together by a central figure. The students also invented and described the people who lived in each house or shop, what they did for a living, their hobbies, and so on. Verbally articulating these social amenities gave them ideas for their pictures, moving the assignment beyond simply drawing an

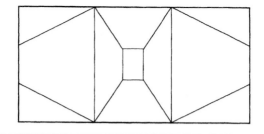

FIGURE 7–11. Perspective skeleton for drawing exterior street scenes.

urban scene to designing a living environment for the real people they had created. It would have been a great lead-in to a topic like Family Life in Postwar Working-Class Britain.

Scott's love of Victorian decor is reflected in his illustration, shown in Figure 7–12. He produces wrought-iron work, Gothic Revival canopies, and decorative finials and explores different kinds of roofing materials and cobblestones. The railway station dominating the right side of his first illustration is full of the embellishments of the age of steam: copious research was needed to produce the accuracy of period engineering design in the signal gantry, the signal box, and the iron bridge. The gable end-of-terrace poster taking up most of the left side is an illustration within an illustration, depicting Blackpool Tower and holiday attractions.

His second illustration centers on the genetically engineered character Zap. A high-tech, futuristic landscape imaginatively fuses the near, middle, and far distances. A wall poster shows an intercity locomotive below the slogan "Relive the Past." With subtle imagination Scott has transformed each of the former buildings into new ones.

Perspective and Writing

The visual force is very strong. As drawing skills improve, so does the desire to raise the narrative level to the pictorial one. The confidence that Steven and Gary found in their "spatial box" illustrations led them to produce an altogether more engaging text than those of their previous books. The complexity of creating a terraced street scene using two-point perspective stimulated Scott to write descriptively about the houses portrayed and their inhabitants: (Part 1) "Hello—my name is Arthur Jackson. . . . Since the war I have cravings for sweets. Mum sends me on errands to the general store which is run by Sam. Mum gives me a silver sixpenny bit to buy Hovis loaves. . . ." (Part 2) "Hi—my name is Zap.

My parents call me this because I was genetically engineered on the Z.A.P.-600 + X9 machine. . . . I travel to my friends on my aerobike. We play on our electro boot hover boards outside and build advanced electronic sets and play on our interplanetary teleport sets inside. An advantage of being genetically engineered is that we do not have to go to school. . . ."

Although the space provided for these descriptions is limited, the discussions and verbal analysis centered on them was anything but confined.

FIGURE 7–12. Scott's two versions of *Jubilee Road*.

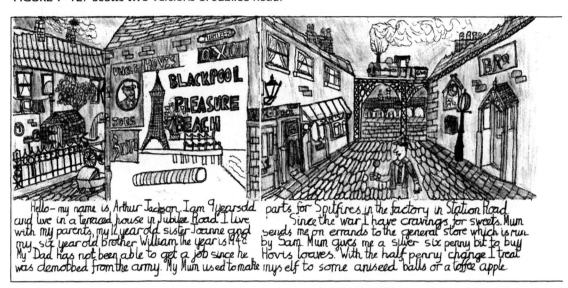

Hello – my name is Arthur Jackson. I am 9 years old and live in a terraced house in Jubilee Road. I live with my parents, my 12 year old sister Joanne and my six year old brother William. The year is 1948. My Dad has not been able to get a job since he was demobbed from the army. My Mum used to make parts for Spitfires in the factory in Station Road. Since the war I have cravings for sweets. Mum sends me on errands to the general store which is run by Sam. Mum gives me a silver six penny bit to buy Hovis loaves. With the half penny change I treat myself to some aniseed balls or a toffee apple.

On the way home I like to stand near the level crossing to watch the steam trains go by and to talk to Jack the station master. Jack likes to tell me tales of when he was in the Home Guard during the war.

John Harthan (1981) argues that illustration has only collective meaning. An illustration standing by itself may possess aesthetic or symbolic merits as a work of art, but it has to be seen as part of a developmental whole— from book cover to cover. Illustration is different from most art activities in school. It is not just that it must evolve side by side with the narrative but that the whole concept demands a developmental strategy unlike the

FIGURE 7–12. Part 2

Hi– my name is Zap. My parents called me this because I was genetically engineered on the Z.AP 600 +X9 machine. I am an only child. To decrease the population there is a law that all parents are only allowed to have one child. My father is an astronaut and flies the shuttle

between Earth and Titon. My mother is a switch board operator for the interplanetary communications network. We live in an apartment on the tenth floor of a housing unit.
I travel to my friends on my aero bike. We play on our electro boot hover boards outside and

build advanced electronic sets and play on our interplanetary teleport sets inside. An advantage of being genetically engineered is that we do not have to go to school. This privilege is granted to children +X9 and above. Tomorrow I start my holiday on a moon off Saturn.

singularity of picture making. Whereas figurative painting "tells a story" in one spatial territory and uses all kinds of techniques to lead the eye from one key point to another, illustration unwinds with the narrative in a linear way, so that images are transformed through imagined time. It is not so much perceiving moments frozen in time, like stills from a film, but holding up (and thus opening up) an indivisible sequence of experiences. Scott's work illustrates this well; he is moving into a new domain of narrative complexity through his growing awareness of the possibilities of perspective.

8

Assessing Words and Pictures

EXPANDING THE VIEW

The success of a piece of writing should be apparent by the effect that it has on its audience.   —NATIONAL WRITING PROJECT (UK)

Intuitive Assessment

Although my emphasis here has been on children as illustrators, the book form affects both the pictorial and the writing process. My primary purpose in having my students make books is so that they will learn to write in a way that the physical parameters of a book demand. At every stage of book making there is a built-in evaluation process designed to get students successfully to the next stage. Without it, it would be impossible for the book to be finished satisfactorily.

Publishing books elevates children's writing to the practice of the professional. While it would be inappropriate to compare child and adult authors qualitatively, the conditions that underpin both, and therefore the assessment procedure, are the same.

While external criticism influences the perceived merits in either case, the arrival at a credible creative statement is, to some degree at least, intuitive. Based on the experience we have had handling materials expressively, we sense when a piece of writing or artwork succeeds and when it does not; we labor at an unfulfilled task until either it wins our approval or it is discarded.

Children possess this intuitive assessment in varying degrees—some barely not at all, many in embryonic form, and others to quite an astonishing degree.

Applied Assessment

Because teachers and students cannot count exclusively on natural insight as a measure of attainment, it is useful to have some common guidelines to ensure continuity of development and progress in learning.

Evaluation as undertaken by a teacher embraces:

- Assessing the teacher's planning and performance.
- Assessing the students' understanding and performance.
- Showing students how they can evaluate their own performance and practice.

Assessing the teacher's planning and performance

Assessing book-art creations, the processes by which they are made, and the students' behavior in making them presupposes that the classroom has been organized into a community of readers, writers, and illustrators engrossed in real tasks.

Teachers need to familiarize themselves with the forms and structures of writing and have an elemental knowledge of picture making and use this understanding to define what they expect from their students. *Do it yourself before asking somebody else to do it* is not a bad dictum in this context.

Teachers might ask themselves the following questions about their performance:

- *Did I prepare the class for the prewriting reflective period?* It is useful if young authors ask themselves what kind of response they want the piece of writing to elicit.
- *How well did I ensure that pupils wrote for a specified audience?* As story ideas are generated students should ask: What makes a good story? Is the "voice" right? Would somebody want to read this? The National Writing Project (1990) asserts that mere secretarial

"corrections" to the text are seldom as effective as changes borne out of a continuous appraisal of audience need.

- *Did I provide an effective working atmosphere?* There are many strategies for organizing a book-art continuum in the classroom—combining whole-class and small-group teaching, using "writing corners," setting up life-drawing sessions (in costume when appropriate), balancing shared and individual writing tasks with large- and small-group discussion, demonstrating on the chalkboard, and introducing visualizing games. Teachers need to assess their own success at stimulating narrative improvisations, discussing strategies, guiding developments, promoting research, extending vocabulary, encouraging teamwork, promoting confidence, providing feedback, encouraging selection and reflection, and fostering discernment and critical acumen.

Assessing the students' understanding and performance

Myra Barrs and Gillian Johnson (1993) explain that grids and checklists have little value as evidence of children's attainments. They favor assessment models (both formative and normative) that enable each student to understand the progress he or she is making and the teacher to identify the stage the student has reached.

Teachers might ask themselves whether students are:

- Developing the ability to assess their own progress.
- Using the basic book form to aid their writing and illustration.
- Planning page sequences to match the word/image concept of the page spread.
- Sharing and collaborating to ensure a healthy self-critical attitude toward writing and illustrating.

In addition teachers can assess students':

- Contribution to group improvisations and discussions.
- Personal and social skills related to collaborative authorship, shared editing and appraising, and presenting the book to an audience.
- Progress in conceiving a narrative; designing a page layout; drafting, editing, and revising; transferring the final draft to the book; and illustrating.

Anne Bauers and John Nichols (1986) question the still widespread practice of responding to young children's texts solely in terms of proofreading rather than striking a balance between what a child has achieved, is attempting to achieve, and cannot yet do. There is evidence to show that as long as children have a reason for doing it, the recursive nature of writing usually leads to successive refinements.

In assessing progress, it is essential that teachers be aware of the stages of development that children pass through in writing and art. (For example, Chapters 6 and 7 show how children develop from elemental spatial schemas to two-point perspective.) Children cannot skip stages but graduate from one stage to the next. Teachers must be aware of a child's level of cognition and any special learning or social difficulties he or she may have in order to enable that child to progress to the next rung of the developmental ladder.

Showing students how they can evaluate their own performance and practice

Children evaluate their own skills through practice, building on each developmental writing and visual event. Lesley Wing Jan (1991) discusses a variety of student record-keeping methods, like work logs, journals, and interactive questionnaires, in which peers, younger children, teachers, and parents can all take part. In journals, children can reflect on their writing and respond to the ideas of others. Questionnaires can ask students what they find difficult or easy about writing, what their strengths and weaknesses are, and more searchingly probe into how pupils might improve their writing style. Children can also comment on their own or colleagues' work in critical reviews, and discuss their own writing in relation to the work of their favorite authors.

The beauty of the basic book form is accessibility; it is relatively easy for pupils to find their way around it, and failings are as identifiable as successes. As they progress through the developmental stages of book art, children should be able to discuss with growing confidence their skills at:

- Sequencing a narrative to match the book form.
- Defining and refining a sentence or group of sentences as an episode.
- Designing narratives so that characters, conflicts, climaxes, and resolutions are structured imaginatively and cogently.
- Cultivating an attractive handwriting style and/or word processing confidently.
- Acquiring the basic secretarial skills of writing.

Assessment in art is a tricky business because of its subjectivity and the philosophical minefield of defining what a work of art is. Margaret

Morgan (1988) has provided some useful guidelines in keeping records describing children's responses to visual resources, the quality of their observational skills, their strengths and weaknesses in mastering techniques, how well they experiment with materials and solve problems. In his visual art assessment model, Rob Barnes (1987) includes empathic response to artwork, clear discussion of ideas, keen environmental observation, and confident use of artistic vocabulary. Records of this kind are particularly useful if the pupils are involved in keeping them. Identifying progress and suggesting change then becomes a two-way process.

Illustrating, of course, has its own criteria within the broader, picture-making ambience of art. I have not gone too far down that road because this is a book for the beginner illustrator, adult and child alike. Chapters 5 and 6 attempt to outline the basic ingredients of figurative picture making, what a "successful" picture comprises, and how this relates to a student's stage of visual development. Illustrations have form and content like the texts they accompany, and, like the texts, can be critically appraised. Artists often use the same nomenclature as writers do, words like *composition* and *grammar*, but they of course mean different things by them.

Through sustained book-art experience students should be able to:

- Express themselves through imaginative and observational drawing.
- Compose lively narrative compositions.
- Bring consistency as well as variety to the sequence of illustrations.
- Relate illustrations inventively to the accompanying text.

Adjusting the Curriculum

The design studio of a publishing house is organized to produce a picture book in the most efficient way possible, with the author, editor, illustrator, and designer working as a team. A model classroom operates in this practical and businesslike way with the same objective—making a book. Alas, in many classrooms learning has become a compromise between opposing educational ideologies. Teachers juggle the demands of conflicting pressures that often originate far from the classroom among people for whom education is solely a political tool. There is nothing in the book-art process that is extracurricular, no new subject to be squeezed in; writing, drawing, and technology have an accepted place in the curriculum. So making books is a matter not of adding to but of reorganizing already established subjects. Time is apportioned to constituent parts of the process according to their status. Clearly, English has priority, but the book arts ensure that visual language is given high status too. That is, after all, how the business and communications world outside the classroom sees it.

A Book to Keep

When children take home a book that they have made at school, parents are delighted and thrilled by it. It is taken ceremoniously from house to house, relative to friend, as an act of celebration ("Look what Sarah made at school!"), and the friends and relatives wish their children came home from school with a books like this too. If parents are "consumers" of the educational system, as they are being identified today, this positive response from parents and children should give a clear signal to teachers that the book-art approach to writing is a good one.

In a journey through a book

it is pleasant to reach

the oasis of a picture or an ornament,

to sit awhile under the palms,

to let our thoughts unburdened stray,

to drink of other intellectual waters,

and to see the ideas we have been pursuing,

perchance, reflecting in them.

Thus we end as we begin, with images.

WALTER CRANE

_____

♦

Appendix: Basic Book Forms

Landscape/Portrait

In general, books are conceived as either of horizontal design (landscape) or vertical design (portrait).

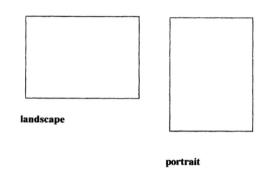

landscape

portrait

Basic Concertina Book

1. Crease sheet of paper into eight rectangles and open.
2. Fold on landscape horizontal.
3. Fold the pages like a concertina to form a book.
4. When opened, the back four pages of the book are necessarily inverted. Since it is a convention of publishing that left-side pages are even numbered, basic books start on page 2.

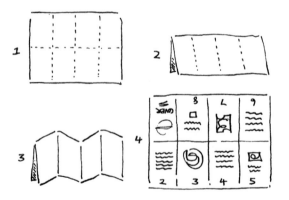

Basic Origami Book

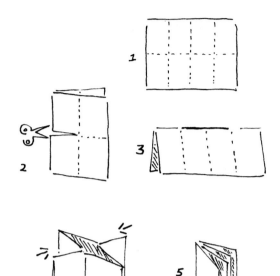

1. Crease sheet of paper into eight rectangles and open.
2. Fold opened sheet in half on the landscape vertical. Cut through double thickness on folded edge from center to fold, as shown.
3. Open sheet and fold on landscape horizontal.
4. Push left and right edges to center forming a cross.
5. Fold panels down to make a six-page book.

The Extended Concertina Book

Strips of paper creased into four pages can simply be added one after the other to create as many pages as required. Students can thus write unrestrictedly and do not have to hold their work to a prescribed model.

Works Cited

Arnheim, Rudolf. 1974. *Art and Visual Perception*. Berkeley, CA: University of California Press.

Barnes, Rob. 1987. *Teaching Art to Young Children 4–9*, pp. 41, 160–70. London: Allen and Unwin.

Barrs, Myra, and Gillian Johnson. 1993. *Record Keeping in the Primary School*, pp. 6–19. London: Hodder & Stoughton.

Bauers, Anne, and John Nichols. 1986. "Early Writing." In *The Writing of Writing*, edited by Andrew Wilkinson, p. 134. Milton Keynes, England: Open University Press.

Beard, Roger. 1984. *Children Writing in the Primary School*, pp. 43–58. London: Hodder & Stoughton.

Bland, David. 1958. *A History of Book Illustration*, p. 88. London: Faber and Faber.

Calkins, Lucy. 1986. *The Art of Teaching Writing*, pp. 117–49. Portsmouth, NH: Heinemann.

Carlin, Eric. 1986. "Writing Development Theory and Practice." In *The Writing of Writing*, edited by Andrew Wilkinson, p. 192. Milton Keynes, England: Open University Press.

Cox, Maureen. 1992. *Children's Drawings*. London: Penguin.

Crane, Walter. 1896. *Of the Decorative Illustration of Books Old and New*, p. 17. London: Bell and Sons.

Edwards, Betty. 1989. *Drawing on the Right Side of the Brain*. Rev. ed., p. 69. Los Angeles: J. P. Tarcher.

Gair, Angela. 1990. *Perspective for Artists*, p. 7. London: Mitchell Beazley.

Gombrich. Ernst. 1952. *The Story of Art*, p. 14. London: Phaidon.

Graham, Judith. 1990. *Pictures on the Page*. Sheffield, England: National Association for the Teaching of English.

Graves, Donald. 1983. *Writing: Teachers and Children at Work*, p. 53–63. Portsmouth, NH: Heinemann.

Hall, Nigel. 1989. *Writing with Reason*, p. ix. London: Hodder & Stoughton.

Halliwell, Susan. 1992. *Teaching English in the Primary Classroom*, p. 7. Harlow, England: Longman.

Harste, Jerome A., Virginia A. Woodward, and Carolyn Burke. 1984. *Language Stories and Literacy Lessons*. Portsmouth, NH: Heinemann.

Harthan, John. 1981. *The Illustrated Book*, p. 257. New York: Thames and Hudson.

Johnson, Paul. 1992. *A Book of One's Own*. Portsmouth, NH: Heinemann. [1990. London: Hodder & Stoughton.]

————. 1993. *Literacy Through the Book Arts*. Portsmouth, NH: Heinemann. [1993. London: Hodder & Stoughton.]

————. 1994. *Books Searching for Authors*. London: Hodder & Stoughton.

Johnson, Pauline. 1990. *Creative Bookbinding*. New York: Dover.

Jordan, Barbara. 1992. "Good for Any Age—Picture Books and the Experienced Reader." In *After Alice*, edited by Morag Styles et al., pp. 113–16. London: Cassell.

Lane, Sheila. 1984. "Learning and Teaching Writing Skills." In *The Education of the Young Child*, edited by David Fontana, pp. 200—213. Oxford, England: Blackwell.

Larson, Gary. 1995. Untitled article. *The Independant Magazine*, December 24, pp. 21–23.

Meek, Margaret. 1992. *On Being Literate*, p. 116. Portsmouth, NH: Heinemann. [1991. London: The Bodley Head.]

Morgan, Margaret. 1988. *Art 4–11*, p. 39. Oxford, England: Basil Blackwell.

Olshansky, Beth. 1994. "Making Writing a Work of Art: Image Making Within the Writing Process." *Language Arts* 71:351.

Shulevitz, Uri. 1985. *Writing with Pictures*. New York: Watson-Guptill.

Watson, Victor. 1992. "The Possibilities of Children's Fiction." In *After Alice*, edited by Morag Styles et al., pp. 11–14. London: Cassell.

Wing Jan, Lesley. 1991. *Write Ways*, pp. 19–21. Melbourne, Australia: Oxford University Press.